BELIEVE IT OR NOT

For Hilary, Sarah and Ben

Patrick Semple

Believe it or not
A MEMOIR

the columba press

First published in 2002 by
the columba press
55A Spruce Avenue, Stillorgan Industrial Park,
Blackrock, Co Dublin
Reprinted 2002.

Cover by Bill Bolger
Cover photograph copyright © Peter Zöller
Origination by The Columba Press
Printed in Ireland by Betaprint, Dublin

ISBN 1 85607 354 8

Acknowledgements
I wish to thank Raymond Refaussé and Michael Burrows for reading the
manuscript. Some names have been changed to preserve anonymity.

Contents

There lives more faith in honest doubt,
believe me, than in half the creeds.

Tennyson
In Memoriam

CHAPTER ONE

Wexford

The Danes founded the town of Wexford, on the south-east coast of Ireland. The name is believed to be the Danish 'Waesfjord' meaning 'white fjord', from the foam-topped waves that broke on the sandbanks at the harbour mouth. Because of these sandbanks the town never developed into a major port. For a short period after the Second World War, however, Wilsons and Staffords, coal merchants, brought in coal in small coasters that arrived and left on a high tide, and even then the dredger might have to make ready the entrance to the harbour.

The town itself is a long narrow Main Street little more than a hundred yards inland from the quay, joined to it by a number of narrow streets. More streets lead upwards to the residential areas. There isn't a wide street in the town itself; at the narrowest point on the Main Street two people each with a heel touching the footpath on either side can shake hands. The centre of the town is the Bull Ring, where there had been bull baiting in earlier times, and in the centre of The Bull Ring stands a monument commemorating the 1798 rebellion with a bronze pikeman on top, known to all as 'the Man in the Bull Ring'. As a child I lived facing the 'Man' over the jeweller's shop which was my father's business.

My family arrived in Wexford when my grandfather was posted there with the army in 1888 and in due course begat a daughter and nine sons. He told a friend that if there were any more boys they'd have to number them! More there might well have been had he not died in 1909, within a few months of the birth of the tenth child, and by the time I was born thirty years later my father was the only one left in the town. The rest were

scattered around the world and, after the war, uncles I didn't
know I had, with wives and some with children, came back to
visit my father and the place of their birth.

The time is the second half of the 1940s – after The Emergency
of gas masks, shortages and ration books. The war itself had
been remote except for news of those from the town who had
joined up. During the war there were some overflights and a
mistaken bombing down the county in Campile. One summer
evening the whole town looked up at the sky full of German aircraft assembling for a raid on some target in Wales or the west of
England. A small child, I remember wondering why so many
airplanes didn't crash into each other. Why German aircraft con-
gregated over the airspace of a neutral country I don't know.
Did the Irish government turn a blind eye or register a protest?
My family, with three members in the British Forces and others
living in England, would have been appalled at any convenience
afforded to the Germans, and I have no doubt that most of the
townspeople would have been appalled too. Equally I have no
doubt there were people, dyed in the wool republicans, who suffered from the delusion that a German victory was in Ireland's
interest.

On a couple of occasions during the war a brother of my
father, who was in British military intelligence, called to us in
Wexford. He was in mufti. He and another man arrived in a
large black car which they parked conspicuously outside our
door. They stayed for tea, and all my uncle would say was that
he was 'on duty'. I learned afterwards that he kept a supply of
petrol in cans in the basement of the house of another of his
brothers in Co Wicklow, who knew no more about his activities
than we did. We discovered years later that the other man was
an engineer and they had been plotting strategic bridges in the
south of Ireland to be mined in the event of a German invasion. I
believe they were operating with the knowledge of the Irish authorities. In England later on during the war, after a car accident
this uncle was unconscious for twenty-six days. As a result of
this he lost permanently his memory of all his wartime activities.

After the war he was awarded an MBE for his military intelligence work and must be unique in having been decorated for something he didn't remember doing!

We listened avidly to BBC broadcasts on the wireless for news of the progress of the war. Then one night my mother came upstairs and woke us:

'The war is over,' she said in great excitement. I sat up and through a haze of sleep asked, 'Did Wexford win?'

The days soon came when young children saw bananas and oranges for the first time, and when tea and sugar and many other rationed commodities became freely available again.

In those days, a fair day was still an event. Farmers got up at three or four o'clock in the morning and walked cattle as much as ten or fifteen miles onto the streets of the town to sell. The following day the fire brigade came out to hose away what the cattle left behind. These were the days of valve radios and before television, when country people came to town to shop by horse and cart or pony and trap, and when cars were so few that children collected car numbers. These were the days when all but a handful of people practised their religion.

My family was Church of Ireland and churchgoing, and Sunday started on Saturday night. My mother left out clean clothes for the morning and did as much preparation for Sunday lunch as possible. When my father came in late from work he cleaned the family's shoes. The Sabbath was to be as work-free as possible. On Sunday mornings, at a quarter past ten, my father would position himself at the foot of the stairs outside the drawing room door, dressed in his grey suit and white shirt, and wait for my older sister and me to present ourselves for inspection.

Having checked hands, shoes and general appearance, he addressed to each in turn the question, 'Have you been?' The excuse, 'I don't need to' elicited not a word from my father but a finger pointing up the stairs where I was inevitably proved wrong.

Mother and father ready, children respectably presented and 'comfortable', we went downstairs, out into the Bull Ring and

walked the short distance along the Main Street, closed and
shuttered after late night opening of the night before, to Saint
Iberius Church where mother and two children made their way
to the family pew while father, a churchwarden, took up his position in the front porch greeting and opening the door for parishioners as they arrived.

Part of a churchwarden's duty in winter was to make sure
the church was warm enough on Sunday morning and to this
end my father lit the solid fuel furnace in the basement early on
Saturday evening, and last thing before going to bed he went
again to check it and fuel it for the night. On Sunday morning he
had already been over to the church before breakfast to check
and fuel it again.

St Iberius Church was broader than it was long. In a
Georgian interior, two Corinthian pillars and two pilasters supported three Romanesque arches to a shallow curved sanctuary.
The broad nave had four short aisles and there was a balcony
round the sides and back of the church. The 'choir', never more
than two or three women and one man, except on special occasions when all and sundry with a note in their heads were
dragooned into service, sat in the protruding curved centre of
the back balcony in front of the organ.

The church was dedicated to St Ibar, who was a fourth-century
saint, which gives the lie to the popular belief that St Patrick first
brought Christianity to Ireland. It would however bring a whole
new perspective if the feast day of the national saint were St Ibar's
day and the motorways of England had been built by Irish Ibys!

The atmosphere of the church was above all of another time;
of the past. Brass nameplates on pews of families long since
dead and gone. No longer were pew rents payable, but parishioners still sat where their fathers and grandfathers sat before
them, and churchwardens were careful to show visitors to free
pews so as not to disturb parishioners in the security of their
family pew. On one occasion I saw visitors who slipped in un-
noticed asked to move to allow a family sit in their own pew –
Christian hospitality!

The past was above all evoked by wall tablets, memorials to dead heroes and paragons of perfection. One was a hero who succumbed to formidable enemies:

Sacred to the memory of Captn. The Honble. John William Hely Hutchinson of the 13th Regt. of Dragoons and of Belmont in this Parish, who died on the 2nd July 1885 in the 25th year of his age at Scutari, where his mortal remains lie under a monument erected by the affection of his Brother Officers. He was called away from the love of all who knew him to die for his Country, by forces more formidable than all the might of Russia, dysentery and fever. This tablet was erected by the agent and tenantry of the estates in this County to express their sorrow for his loss, but not as those who have no hope, trusting in the promise 'He that liveth and believeth in me shall never die.'

Another was a local hero:

Sacred to the memory of the late Charles Vallotton, Esq. A major in the Army and a Capt. in the 56th Regt. Of Infantry who in the Suburbs on the 11th of July 1793 when zealously co-operating with the Civil Power in support of the mild and beneficent laws of his country, received a mortal wound from a savage hand. Thus untimely fell this accomplished Gentleman not less admired and beloved for every social quality than he was eminently distinguished on every occasion by the enterprise and gallantry of a soldier. Reader, lament with every good man the irreparable loss and strive to emulate his many virtues. The Corporation of Wexford, with becoming gratitude, erected this monument to perpetuate their high respect for his inestimable character.

And another was a paragon of virtue and of beauty:

Sacred to the memory of Mrs Elizabeth Ogle, a more than loved sister and a faultless friend. Her mind was as pure and angelical as her form was beautiful. If a human being could be perfect she was perfect. She was as truly beloved and esteemed as she is universally lamented by all those who knew her. And unceasingly so by her ever sorrowing sister Jane

Moore, who to indulge her unabated grief , erects this humble tribute to her matchless worth in the month of June 1815.
Obit 11th August 1807.

The tablets were simple plaques, elaborate scrolls, a bust of the
virtuous deceased and one large sculptured representation of a
nineteenth-century warship on which the unfortunate parishioner had lost his life in a battle at sea. There were no tablets to
servants or tradesmen.

On an average Sunday less than a quarter of the pews on the
ground floor were occupied and there was nobody in the balcony except the choir – no more than forty or fifty people, a remnant of what would have been a full church at the end of the last
century, forty or fifty years previously.

In our pew I sat on the inside beside my sister, who took it
upon herself to make sure I paid attention and did the right
thing at the right time not to disgrace the family, since an important part of being in church was to be respectable. Behaving well,
even for a small boy, was the thing. What other people thought
was important. If I misbehaved I was put sitting between my
mother and father and so I learned to move quietly in order to
keep the freedom of the inside of the pew.

Standing, I could just about see over the top of the pew, so
kneeling I couldn't see at all and would turn around and sit on
the moth-eaten kneeler with stuffing coming out, facing back-
wards, and lean my elbows on the seat for the duration of the
prayers. This was acceptable since there was nobody in the pew
behind, and provided I was quiet and couldn't be seen. I knew
some of the hymns from school but the sermons were endless.
One curate, when he went into the pulpit, took off his watch and
placed it on the stand in front of him, whether to make sure he
went on long enough or didn't go on too long I'm not sure. For
me the sermons were always too long, and for adults too I have
no doubt, if they were honest enough to admit it. I couldn't wait
for 'And now to God the Father, God the Son and God the Holy
Ghost ...' when everyone stood up for the last hymn and my
mother would pass me the silver threepenny bit with the hare or

the brown one with the twelve sides for the collection, which coin had been stopped, unfairly I thought, out of my pocket money of a shilling.

On one Sunday in the month the service was Morning Prayer with Holy Communion tacked on at the end. Morning Prayer was shortened and when it ended those who weren't staying for Communion, and this included all the children, left. For those leaving this meant a fifty-minute service rather than the usual hour or more.

I knew most of the other families in church on Sunday mornings. The Sherwoods sat at the far side of the church from us. Joe Sherwood, home from the war, sat with his schoolteacher sister Miss Mary and sometimes Miss Lizzie. For much of the war Joe's family had no news of him, until at the end of the war he was released from a Japanese prisoner-of-war camp. He was sent to Canada to recover but he wasn't the same and he never worked again. He was kindly and gentle and said very little. He turned up from time to time at school to do handyman jobs for Mary. He had a small boat at the Crescent Quay and fished in the harbour during the summer. Lizzie, Joe and Mary's sister, who kept house for the three, was particularly kind to children and a child sent on a message from school to the Sherwood house in Parnell Street never returned without a biscuit. Mary too, outside school, was kind and gentle and always spoke to her children. In school she was pleasant most of the time, but occasionally lost her temper, when she became, as the senior boys would say, 'a walkin' divil'.

Near the Sherwoods sat the Elgees, Edith and her father John. John was a second cousin of Oscar Wilde. Speranza, Oscar Wilde's mother was a grand-daughter of Archdeacon Elgee, a former rector of the parish. John Elgee was a solicitor and a martinet who didn't like to be reminded of his relationship to, as he would have seen it, his infamous cousin. He had had four children but one had been drowned in a yachting accident. The survivors were Edith, Frances and Dick. (Richard to the family.) When his wife died Miss Edith came home from her teaching job in Dublin to look after her father and brother.

Miss Frances had gone to England. Dick, a solicitor too, worked with his father who allowed him to do little more than post the letters, and so he lost interest. He spent his time sailing and playing cricket in the summer and playing hockey in the winter. Unlike his father and Edith who never missed, he never appeared in church. When his father died Dick dressed in tails for the duration of the obsequies, and cut a fine dash as he walked along the Main Street from Selskar, where the Elgees lived, to the North Station to meet Frances coming home from England.

Edith returned to teaching in Dublin after her father's death. She was a tall mannish woman, bossy but kindly, more at ease with children than adults. She retired to Wexford, and lived alone until she died.

Minorities tend to diminish. The less than 5% Protestant minority in the south cannot afford families that don't procreate, like the Sherwoods and the Elgees, or that marry Roman Catholics and bring their children up as Catholics. I know of one Protestant woman who upbraided another who had no children for not doing her bit for the Protestant community. It never occurred to her that the woman she upbraided dearly wanted children, not to boost Protestant numbers, but for their own sake.

The Elgees were a distinguished Protestant family, one member of which as we have seen was Oscar Wilde, and another was an admiral McClure who discovered the North West Passage. There were no children, so they simply died out. Sometimes we human beings forget how much we are at the mercy of nature and ultimately how little say we have.

In many Church of Ireland parish churches, lay people read the lessons in church. This naturally requires a certain level of confidence, literacy and a likelihood of being heard, which combination was found among members of the aristocracy, retired colonels and sundry others of the gentry and officer class, almost always male. One of these, Colonel French, recently returned from the war, sat some pews in front of us in St Iberius. During school holidays three sons in their teens appeared in church with him. All four were six foot plus and to me looked like giants of men. The Colonel's wife died and in due course he married his brother's widow and, as it were, kept it all in the family. Colonel French was also head and tail of the Select Vestry, the committee of the parish responsible for parochial matters temporal.

In earlier years the nobility and gentry largely ran the administrative end of the life of the Church of Ireland at national, diocesan and parish level. They also, be it said, often provided finance at local level. Today in many parishes, members of this social group still exercise influence, some for the good, but some of them behave as 'godfathers', making life difficult for the rector.

Mrs Levingston sat across the aisle from us with her two young boys. Her husband, an electrician who drove an old Austin 'matchbox', never went to church. She was a large round woman who, when she spoke, smiled quizzically. She ran the retail end of the business in their small electrical shop on Common Quay Street. The shop was so small that when she emerged from the living quarters at the back to serve a customer, she could hardly be seen behind cartons of electrical appliances piled high on the floor and on the counter. She was nonetheless a keen businesswoman and, later on, when the rector was trying to convince her to let her elder boy go to university, she floored him with: 'Weren't you at university and you don't even own the house you live in.'

Around this time some 'ordinary' parishioners were beginning to read lessons too. One of these was Sam Coe who was virtually indestructible. During his life he had a number of almost fatal accidents and illnesses before he finally succumbed at the age of ninety, having fallen off a ladder painting the upstairs windows of his house while his wife was away. Colonel French and Sam read equally well in church and when the Colonel read the first lesson and Sam the second the noticeable contrast was not between the Old and New Testaments but between their accents – the Colonel's a west British public school accent and Sam's an ordinary Wexford accent.

There is a perception amongst Roman Catholics that there are no poor Protestants in the south. This is not true. There are so few Protestants that the poor ones are probably less noticeable. Anyway, how would one expect to know an impoverished Protestant from an impoverished Catholic? The misconception arises from the perception of Protestants as Anglo-Irish – Brendan Behan's 'Protestant with a horse.' I have no doubt that Protestants are represented proportionately in every stratum of society.

In many Church of Ireland congregations you find one parishioner who sings louder than everyone else. This is especially true in small congregations. We had one in St Iberius. She sat over to the right of us under the balcony, which probably exaggerated her excessive volume. How her daughter felt when her mother sang the hymns on the top of her voice I don't know but embarrassment may have accounted for the fact that her husband seldom appeared in church with his wife and daughter but usually came in the evening on his own. It may, however, have been because he worked late on Saturday night.

Today, fifty or so years later, no members of any of these, and of many other families of the time, attend St Iberius. Some families have died out, others have moved. In one case the sole survivor is too old to attend and another lone survivor does not attend.

The rector was The Reverend John Eldon Hazley. Like most if not all Church of Ireland clergy of the time, he trained for the ministry at Trinity College Dublin, where the Divinity School was exclusively Anglican. In those days God only called to ordination in the Church of Ireland those who could matriculate and afford to attend Trinity to read for a degree and proceed to the Divinity School. Others could become Sunday School teachers and prominent laymen. None the less, there were more men ordained than there were vacancies for them in the Church of Ireland and some had to go to England or abroad for curacies.

Canon Hazley was affable, kind and good but, as was probably the case with most clergy in those days, he was largely untouched by the ways of the wicked world. My mother recounted that on the night that I was born he called to the house and after one glass of sherry broke into 'Run Rabbit, Run Rabbit, Run Run Run'. He was of medium height, slight, round-shouldered and wore his thin black hair sleeked down on his head. During the week he cycled around the parish on a bicycle with a leather attache case on the carrier. He eventually learned to drive and no longer needed a hackney car on Sunday mornings to take him from the town out to Rathaspeck to take the service there, but he still used the bike around town.

These were the days of Catholic triumphalism when ecumenism in provincial Ireland was non-existent. Relations between individuals and families were good but at a parish level there was no contact. Nationalism and its accompanying Catholicism had been in the ascendancy for only twenty or thirty years. The Protestant community was so small it was virtually ignored and, from a Catholic point of view, we were all going to hell anyway. Some few Protestants did not withdraw and keep their heads down but played their civic part. For example, Dr Hadden, a retired lay Methodist Missionary, was a member of Wexford Corporation, and my father joined the Local Defence Force during the war. These, however, were the exceptions. On the other hand, one Catholic family, after a disagreement with the Catholic authorities, sent their children to the Church of Ireland National School – a brave thing to do in those days. Canon Hazley would have had no contact with the Catholic clergy and if they met in public they would simply have exchanged polite greetings and passed on.

Canon Hazley was married without children and Mrs Hazley performed the tasks customary to a rector's wife. First of all she appeared in church every Sunday and on other occasions when there was a service. She was the chief officer of the Mothers' Union that met in the rectory and she was unpaid secretary and general helper and supporter of her husband on parish occasions.

The Sunday morning service was much more than a meeting

for the worship of Almighty God according to the Anglican tradition, it was the coming together of a tiny minority affirming their distinctiveness and their determination to survive. What was distinctive from the majority Roman Catholic community was never mentioned; it was not overt and would not have been understood by most attenders at St Iberius except in a very simple way. There was no sense in which I experienced anything anti-Roman Catholic; on the contrary, in my family there was admiration for the diligence of Catholics in attending to religious duties, many of which were not observed in our church. There was a strong sense of allegiance, however, to the Church of Ireland, which was more 'tribal' than theological.

There was an awareness of being different. How could it have been otherwise when 95% of the population of the town went to one of three other churches? Roman Catholic churches in those days were still called 'chapels', a hangover from the days when the Church of Ireland was the established church and the Roman Catholic Church was sometimes referred to offensively as the Roman Mission in Ireland! Technically the Methodist and Presbyterian churches, not being of the established church, should also have been called chapels, but I don't believe they were.

As for distinctiveness from Methodists and Presbyterians, one was aware that there must have been some differences but I had no idea what they were, and anyway they were too few in number to notice very much, which was how Roman Catholics felt about the rest of us.

Relations with our Roman Catholic friends and neighbours were not an issue. They were as unexceptional as relations between friends and neighbours anywhere, and one was not aware of religious difference most of the time, except when streams of people walked up the Main Street to one of the three chapels on saints' days observed by the Catholic Church and not by the Church of Ireland, and for Sodalities and Missions. These were the times that one was aware of difference. There were occasional encounters too with children who might stop me on the town and say something like:

'Aren't you a Protestant?'

'Yes, I am.'

'Well, you're going to hell. All Protestants go to hell. Only Catholics go to heaven.'

This led to a suspicion on the part of a small boy that there was some kind of difference!

When I eventually asked my mother about this she told me my informants were wrong and not to mind them, because everybody who loved God and did what was right would go to heaven. I was quite happy and reassured by my mother's answer, but I did wonder at the unmistakeable tone of authority with which the other children had told me, and I did wonder who their informants had been.

In our family Sunday church was as much part of life as breathing. You would have to be very sick to miss it. With so few in church it was easy to notice who was there and who was not. There were some who were 'out' only occasionally and I used to wonder what brought them out one Sunday and not another, and there were two couples, both good friends of my parents, who never went to church at all. They were part of the tribe, but they didn't attend the ritual, and as far as I could see they were none the worse for it, but then of course I couldn't see into their immortal souls and, apart from that, it was none of my, nor anybody else's, business that they didn't go to church. That's what it's like to be a Protestant – having the freedom to make up your own mind. Freedom of conscience is essential to Protestantism. You may dissent from the ritual, but the Protestant 'mortaler' was to dissent from the tribe – to become a Catholic or to marry a Catholic and bring your children up as Catholics. Protestants tended to socialise with Protestants, but not exclusively. Communities exist around events and the Protestant community was most itself at the services of the church.

For us children it wasn't the end of it when church was over. There was Sunday School, which took place in the other Church of Ireland church in the town, Selskar Abbey. Why, when we couldn't even quarter fill one church, we needed a second one I don't know; well I do really, and it wasn't to hold Sunday School in. As the former established church, history bequeathed us two churches and we were going to hold on to them – at all costs, and cost it probably did, for proper maintenance of old churches is an expensive business. Apart from Sunday School, Selskar was used for mid-week Lenten services and Harvest Thanksgivings, because it was easier and cheaper to heat than Saint Iberius. It was also used for Evening Prayer in the winter during the war, as the lights of St Iberius could be seen at sea.

At the end of the morning service at Saint Iberius, Miss Elgee and Mr Coe mustered all the children, six or eight or perhaps ten on a good day, and with Miss Elgee taking two of the smallest by the hand led us up Cornmarket along Abbey Street to Selskar. Mr Coe carried the keys – one to the padlock on the gate and an enormous one to the door of the church that two of the senior boys were allowed to open. Opening locks it seems was men's work. Inside the two teachers sat in pews on either side of the aisle, Mr Coe taking the seniors and Miss Elgee the juniors. Miss Elgee taught New Testament bible stories from memory while Mr Coe taught the Old Testament from his well-thumbed bible. This lasted for the best part of half an hour and then a dash for the gate and home. There were no volunteers for locking up.

When my sister and I arrived home, Sunday lunch, a roast joint, was ready and all four sat down, still in Sunday best, to the most formal meal of the week. Grace was always said and there was always dessert. Family lunch was part of the Sunday ritual. My parents quizzed Ann and me to know what we had done at Sunday School, and we were expected to give a reasonable account of what we had learned.

One summer Sunday, during Sunday School holidays, I pleaded with my parents and was allowed to go back to a friend's house at the other end of the town after church. The condition was that I would be home in time for lunch. To be late for any meal was serious, but to be late for Sunday lunch was unthinkable. It was the one day in the week when it was predictable that my father's business could not prevent him being present with the rest of the family. Needless to say, I left my friend's house at the last minute and ran like a hare along the deserted Main Street. In the distance I heard singing that was getting louder, and before I knew it I was confronted with a huge crowd of people, the width of the street, moving slowly towards me, blocking my way.

I slowed to a walk and approached cautiously. Two priests fully robed led the procession. Four men held aloft on poles an ornately draped square platform on which was what looked to me like a silver stand surrounded by sunrays. A hood covered the platform, from the corners of which hung white ropes with tassels held by four boys in cottas and soutanes. My surprise and interest were tempered by my need to pass quickly, but there was no way through.

I moved into the side as the procession came closer and was slowly swallowed up as I tried to make headway against the tide. When I was about two thirds way through the crowd, the singing suddenly stopped and to my horror everyone dropped to their knees, leaving me alone standing, faced in the opposite direction. As the prayers began I had two options, to stand still or to pick my way as inconspicuously as possible through the kneeling crowd. I decided on the latter and had no sooner squeezed past the person nearest me when there was a tug on my jacket from below that almost pulled me over. I reclaimed my jacket and stayed standing. I stood my ground while the prayers droned on interminably. When they finally ended and everyone stood up, I pushed my way to the back and ran for home. Rather than my undoing, the procession had been my saving. My parents had seen it pass and excused my lateness because of it.

Apart from church and lunch, Sunday was a very different day from any other in the week. As many chores as possible, such as shoe cleaning and food preparation, were done on Saturday night. We children were not allowed to take out our bicycles on Sunday or to call for friends or to have friends in. We had to play quietly in our bedrooms, not in the drawing room

where my father slept for what seemed like most of the afternoon. My mother would never sew or knit on Sunday – to do so
was to violate the Sabbath: 'What you sew on Sunday you'll rip
on Monday.' We were certainly not allowed to play cards, however we could play Lexicon, a card game with letters, which had
no connection whatever with the devil.

Quietness and sedateness were the principles for Sunday activities. Later in the afternoon, weather permitting, we might go
for a walk, children in front, parents behind. In summer we
might even walk to Park and watch cricket, and when I was
older I could play. Somehow cricket was allowed, but to watch
or play football on Sunday was out of the question!

There was Evening Prayer at 7.00pm. One or more of our
family went from time to time. In earlier days this was the service to which the servants who had to work in the morning
went, having left a cold collation for the family. Those were the
days of those commemorated on the wall tablets, but there was
only a handful of people at St Iberius in the evening now – a few
who missed the morning service, a few worthy or lonely souls
who were at church for the second time on Sunday and a few
who went only in the evening. There was something comforting,
especially on a dark winter's night, about Evening Prayer from
the *Book of Common Prayer*: *Magnificat*, *Nunc Dimittis* and the
evening collects: '...Give unto thy servants that peace which the
world cannot give … that we being defended from the fear of
our enemies may pass our time in rest and quietness,' and
'Lighten our darkness, we beseech thee, O Lord, and by thy
great mercy defend us from all perils and dangers of this night,
for the love of thy only Son our Saviour, Jesus Christ.'

The *Book of Common Prayer* contained all the services of the
church: Morning and Evening Prayer, forms for the administration of the sacraments and other occasional rites. Cranmer was
the original inspiration, in the early Reformation period, for the
production of a book in English for the use of priest and people.
After about one hundred years it settled into a form that has remained virtually unchanged since 1662. One of the main reasons

for its production was to make the services of the church available in English in order that the people might understand them.

The Tudor English of the *BCP* is beautiful and much loved by the people of the Church of Ireland, but it was no longer the English of the people by the middle of the twentieth century. Some of the theological concepts used were also out of date, at least for thinking people. For example, the idea in the prayers for rain or for fair weather that it was reasonable to pray to God to intervene in the weather to suit our purposes was no longer credible. The *BCP* prayer for a sick person prays that God will 'sanctify this thy fatherly correction to him'. In other words, that physical illness is a punishment of God from which the unfortunate sufferer might learn for the future.

In the mid 1960s the church began to produce revised liturgies that have largely replaced the *BCP* in common usage, though in theory they were designed for use in parallel with it. Today the *BCP* has diminished in use and in some places disappeared altogether, much to the regret of some church members. This is similar to the regret of many Catholics after Vatican II for the loss of the Latin Mass.

The Protestant population of Wexford was probably about the national average, something under five per cent, so there was an inevitable sense of the all-pervasive influence of the Catholic Church. There were statues and Catholic Church holidays, priests and brothers were saluted in public and, from time to time, religious processions were held on the streets. On the face of it this did not bother Protestants, but there were under the surface strong tribal loyalties that erupted from time to time. One Sunday morning going out to church, written in large letters on the footpath across the front of our shop and the shop next door, owned by a Presbyterian family, was the word 'boycott'. What provoked it we had no idea. Later there was the infamous Fethard-on-Sea case when a whole community was divided bitterly over the education of the children of a mixed marriage.

Insofar as the Protestant community stood apart, it was for fear of mixed marriages and the feeling that at the slightest opportunity Catholics would want to try to convert them. There were, however, hints that for Protestants their spiritual home was England – that since the formation of the State Protestants had been somehow cut off from England and were a besieged minority. I had no sense whatever of this growing up. However, when Catholic and Irish seemed indivisible, Protestants would want to protest that they were Protestant and Irish, but certainly none the less Irish. I believe that this was true and still is for most Protestants living in the south. In school Miss Sherwood taught us that the two things one stood to attention for were the Creed and the National Anthem.

Since Protestants were, from a Catholic point of view, destined for hell, I suppose it was understandable that the Protestant partner to a prospective mixed marriage should be put under the severest pressure to convert to Roman Catholicism, either for genuine concern for the well-being of his or her soul or for fear that they might adversely affect the Catholic allegiance or the religious practice of their spouse. Some Protestants in those days for this reason did become Roman Catholics before mixed marriages, and for those who didn't it meant an early morning marriage in the sacristy of the Catholic Church with those present restricted to two witnesses. In this case, by the decree *Ne Temere*, both partners had to sign a document promising to bring up all children of the marriage as Roman Catholics.

Protestants should remember, however, before they feel too self-righteous about this draconian regulation, that in previous generations their forefathers made it illegal by infinitely more draconian laws for Roman Catholics to practise their religion at all, when they had to resort to the hills and the forests to celebrate Mass. They were limited in the property they could own and barred from keeping Catholic schools and barred from some of the professions. The remnants of these Penal Laws were abolished no more than a couple of generations before. The Roman Catholic Bishop of Killaloe recently apologised for the effects and inflexible application of *Ne Temere*. As far as I know nobody has officially expressed regret for the Penal Laws.

Before the Catholic Church decree *Ne Temere* of 1907, there was in Ireland a fair and sensible practice by which sons of a mixed marriage were brought up in the religion of their father and daughters in their mother's religion. There was a natural fairness overall about this custom, but the effects of *Ne Temere* became a major contribution to the decimation of the Protestants of the southern State. Apart from the flight of many Protestant families to Northern Ireland and England after the formation of the State for fear of reprisals, *Ne Temere* was the chief reason for the steady decline of Protestant numbers in the south. There is hardly a Protestant family in the south that was not affected by this unjust decree.

Ne Temere has now been replaced in the Roman Catholic Church by more reasonable regulations which allow an inter-church marriage to take place in a Protestant Church without the necessary presence of a Catholic priest, though one is usually invited and normally attends. The Protestant partner is not asked to make any promises and the Roman Catholic partner promises only to do all in their power to bring up their children as Roman Catholics, and taking account of the Protestant part-ner's conscience this can be interpreted liberally depending on the Catholic priest involved.

This was the background against which the little Church of Ireland community of Wexford of the time, and every other Church of Ireland community around the south of Ireland, lived. Survival of the group was the name of the game and many characteristic Protestant attitudes and practices developed in order to ensure that the insidious effects of *Ne Temere* were kept to a minimum. These effects were felt most acutely in rural com-munities where the mystique of land was deep in the bones of farmers and where a Protestant farm could become a Catholic farm in one generation. To avoid this it was not uncommon for a son to be disinherited if he married a Roman Catholic.

Church of Ireland parishes ran 'Socials' which were publicised by announcement in the church of the host parish and in the churches of neighbouring parishes. They were in effect dances for Protestants to meet Protestants in order to avoid the effects of *Ne Temere*. Catholics could be forgiven for seeing these socials as positively exclusive religiously or socially, whereas they were, rather, defensive. The average Roman Catholic would have known nothing about *Ne Temere* and its effects on the small Protestant community unless they had some involvement in a mixed marriage, and anyhow some would probably have felt it not unreasonable in the circumstances that a Protestant should convert to the 'one true church'. Human nature being what it is there were, of course, some Protestants who were glad of the exclusiveness of these all-Protestant socials.

These were the days when some Protestant firms would employ only Protestants to apprenticeships and to management. Hadden's drapery shop was one such. They did, however, employ Catholics as messenger boys in their shop and workers in their factory. Protestant young people came from all over Ireland to apprenticeships in Hadden's, who while training them in their trade were *in loco parentis* and responsible for their spiritual and moral welfare. Apprentices had to be in at a certain time at night and if they wanted to attend a suitable Protestant social they had to apply for a 'late key'. Just like parents in whose *locus* they were, there was only so much spiritual and moral policing they could do. One thing they did, however, was insist that apprentices went to church and to this end there was a Hadden's pew in St Iberius Church which was never overcrowded.

Their social life did, however, rotate around the YMCA which was the social and recreational arm of the parish. It provided a billiard table, badminton, table tennis, amateur dramatics and a reading room. It was here in the bosom of the local parish that parents were reassured that their sons and daughters would meet nice respectable Protestants and so avoid the problem of mixed marriages.

The chief instruments for the maintenance of religious control, of course, were denominational schools. Roman Catholic children were indoctrinated in Roman Catholic managed schools and Church of Ireland children were indoctrinated in

Church of Ireland managed schools. Depending on your own perspective or experience, you can choose whether to understand the word 'indoctrinate' in a pejorative sense or not. Diocesan priests and religious orders of nuns and brothers staffed the Catholic schools of Wexford, while the Church of Ireland schools, primary and secondary, were staffed by lay people. In the schools of both traditions, religious education was taught and both would claim, through the atmosphere of their schools, to communicate to their pupils their own distinctive ethos. For this reason both churches are still determined to hold on to church managed schools at all costs. The clergy in fact pay the chief price for the maintenance of church schools in both traditions. So great is the work load in managing schools and the stress of coping with problems caused by parents, teachers and children, that some Church of Ireland clergy will not allow their names to be considered for appointment to parishes with primary schools. Others, however, support them strongly as the means of preserving the Church of Ireland ethos in the Republic.

CHAPTER TWO

No 4 National School

No 4 National School Wexford was behind a door in the wall in the corner of St Patrick's Square. It was a single large rectangular room with a high ceiling and a sawdust stove at the far end. There were three big sash windows on the long south-facing wall and one small circular window high up on the north side. The small desks were at the front near the stove and the teacher's desk, while the bigger ones were behind them further back towards the door. Most of the wall space was covered with old maps and posters.

Miss Sherwood was a small stocky figure with bushy eye-brows. Her mousy hair, going grey, was drawn into a bun at the back, leaving wisps flying in all directions. She wore jumpers, cardigans and heavy tweed skirts, with comfortable walking shoes loosely laced. She was a martyr to corns and walked with a slightly hesitant gait that the country boys described as 'bad on the feet'. She had a gentle voice that she had no difficulty raising when the need arose. On one occasion she lost her temper and caned a boy with such vigour that her bun fell apart. She ignored it until the caning was finished, and in a silence that turned every tick of the clock into a hammer blow, she retreated to her high desk on the platform in the corner, and regaining her composure, remade her bun. Only the brave dared raise their heads to look.

Mary, as we called her behind her back, had trained before the formation of the State and had availed of one of the special courses for teachers to learn Irish. She not only learned it, she became an enthusiast for the language, and communicated her love of Irish to some of her pupils. She taught it by using it at every opportunity, but most of her pupils positively disliked it.

In winter Mary had a permanent drip on the end of her nose. Without interrupting her teaching she could slip her hand under the hem of her skirt, take a handkerchief from the leg of her knickers, wipe the drip and return the hankie in a wink.

She had eight classes to teach, junior infants to sixth class. The class she was teaching stood at the top of the room and with her back to the blackboard and easel, compass like, she drew a semi-circle with chalk on the floor. The knots protruding from the floorboards, worn down by generations of children's feet, inevitably broke the chalk at least once during this operation, to the barely concealed amusement of the pupils, who when she had completed the semi-circle, toed the line while she stood beside the blackboard and conducted the class. These classes were frequently interrupted by Mary shouting at pupils down the room who were not concentrating on the work she had set them to do.

Over the wall of the school yard there was a derelict graveyard that had for the children a certain sinister mystique. During football at breaktime, when the ball went over the wall into the graveyard one of the bigger boys would retrieve it, often with stories of bodies and bones.

One fine summer morning I arrived into school before anyone else was there. I left my schoolbag at the door, went to the top of the playground, climbed the wall of the graveyard and peered over the top. All I could see was a wilderness of tall grass, nettles and briars, so I climbed onto the top of the wall from where I could see some gravestones. I jumped down and stood absolutely still. Then I pushed my way slowly through the grass onto an overgrown path. There were no bodies, bones or open graves, so I wandered from one leaning headstone to another, absorbed into the stillness of the place. I could feel the warmth of the sun on my back. I was lost in another world. Suddenly the silence was broken by a noise from the school yard. I stood and listened. There were voices. I ran back quickly, avoiding as best I could the big clumps of grass and nettle and the long tentacles of briar, and climbed onto the wall. Below me stood Mary with a face like thunder, and behind her a group of children looking up.

'Come down here at once!' She shouted.

I jumped off the wall and fell in a heap on the ground in front of her.

'Get up.'

I got to my feet.

'What were you doing in there?'

'Reading.'

'Reading?'

'I was reading the headstones.'

Without warning Mary took a swipe at my legs. The other children backed away. The slap stung my bare calf, already scratched and stung.

'Don't ever get up on that wall again,' she shouted pointing up with her right index finger, the first joint of which was permanently dislocated at an angle of 45 degrees, so that when she pointed at the wall she was pointing at me and when she pointed at me she was pointing at the ground.

'Go inside,' she added and strode down the yard as firmly as her corns allowed.

Despite its ending, I had enjoyed my adventure and learned in passing that the living are more to be feared than the dead.

When she was in good humour, Mary sometimes gave jobs like topping up inkwells to senior pupils. Occasionally we had to wash them all and make fresh ink. We took the wells from the desks, emptied out the dregs, and put them in a bucket of water to soak. While they were soaking, we measured ink powder into an old jug kept for the purpose, added water, stirred it thoroughly and poured it into the clean inkwells back in the desks. The ink fuelled the pens used to write headline copies:

'A rolling stone gathers no moss.'

'A stitch in time saves nine.'

Lightly on the up stroke and heavy on the down.

Ink was the bane of my life at school. I could not understand why, no matter how careful I was, it climbed up the nib and all over my fingers. It was good fun making fingerprints on scraps of paper, but when it got onto the page it meant trouble.

In winter the big sawdust stove, with the chimney going up through the ceiling, kept the schoolroom warm even in the coldest weather. It had replaced a coal burning stove when coal became scarce or unavailable during the war, since there was a ready supply of sawdust from Hadden's furniture factory in the town.

In the morning the first of the bigger boys to arrive into school went up to the shed in the yard and brought down two large buckets of sawdust. He packed it firmly into the stove around a thick vertical pole which he removed when the sawdust was within an inch or two of the top, and replaced the cover. Mary then took over. She opened a little door at the bottom that gave access to the area under the floor of the stove. In the top of this compartment was a hole the circumference of the pole through which it had come when the stove was being filled. Into this she placed a roll of tightly wound newspaper soaked in paraffin, lit it and closed the door. The flame went up the funnel left by the pole and ignited the sawdust. In no time at all the stove was red and the room was warm. It was still hot enough at lunchtime to boil water to dilute Bovril and Oxo cubes for children who stayed for lunch.

I was familiar with country people who came to town for fair days. At school I discovered children of these tanned and rugged people. They wore boots instead of shoes and somehow conveyed the impression that their time in school was a bothersome interruption to the real purpose of life, farming. At certain seasons of the year their attendance was fitful, when some stayed at home to help with the seasonal work in hand. At these busy times two or three brothers in a family might take it in turn to attend school making the 'townies' envious and making Mary furious.

The 'countries' came to No 4 School under a Church of Ireland scheme to enable children from outside the town to attend a school of their own denomination. They were collected and brought in in the mornings by hackney car, and as often as not they were late, for which Mary blamed the driver, but she would hold off calling the roll until they arrived. This led to a running battle between Mary and the driver, who in turn blamed some of the children for not being at their meeting point on time. To get her own back on the driver Mary would sometimes keep the school in late in the afternoon, and at about five past three the driver would knock on the door. This knock Mary ignored. A few minutes later the driver would knock again and put his head around to be greeted with a tirade to the effect that if he had had the children in on time in the morning they could leave on time in the afternoon. The townies of course were the innocent victims of this unseemly 'war'.

These were the days before child locks and safety belts, when one day on the way home in the countries' car the driver became aware of whispering in the back. He looked in his mirror and asked where was Joe. The reply came back that he had fallen out back the road a bit. He had, in fact, fallen out and was badly injured but in due course he recovered and returned to school something of a hero.

Mary taught religious education that largely amounted to New Testament bible stories for the juniors and Old Testament for the seniors, and we learned some of the well known children's hymns:

Jesus loves me this I know,
For the Bible tells me so;
Little ones to him belong,
They are weak but he is strong.

Jesus bids us shine with a pure, clear light
Like a little candle burning in the night;
In this world of darkness so we must shine,
You in your small corner and I in mine.
And the favourite of them all:
All things bright and beautiful,
All creatures great and small,

All things wise and wonderful,
The Lord God made them all.

No more than my parents, or any other teacher I had later on, would Mary make a critical comment on any other religion. She taught us the Christian faith simply and practically according to the tradition of the Church of Ireland and she was a natural ecumenist before the word was invented. She was also a strong nationalist with a small 'n'. She taught us to be proud of, and to honour our country. For her age and generation and with her first name 'Victoria', she was broad minded, tolerant (except for late hackney drivers!) and a very modern woman.

Canon Hazley called to the school at least once a week. His visits were irregular, but always in the morning. When he came in, all the pupils stood up and in sing-song unison intoned 'Good morning, Canon Hazley'. He didn't come to teach and when he arrived Mary would tell us to get on with our work and the two would retire to her high desk on the platform in the corner to talk. The noise level rose steadily as pupils' concentration waned and Mary would either step down from the platform and wither the whole room to silence with a look, or ring the bell to let us out to play. Needless to say, the longer Canon Hazley stayed the better we liked it.

In June the Diocesan Board of Education held Religious Knowledge exams and for our school these took place in Selskar Abbey. The examiners were clergy from around the diocese. To me some of them looked like ordinary men dressed up as clergy and one small fat man with a shock of red hair looked to me no more like a clergyman than the man in the moon.

The exams were oral and the candidates sat in pews by class with the examiner facing them from the pew in front asking questions along the row. Some of the clergy were friendly and kind and gave hints or changed questions to help a puzzled child; some would do anything to help a child come up with an answer, while others were hard-hearted sticklers who accepted only the precise answer they wanted. Some children were bright and answered quickly while others did much head tapping and

some even cried when they couldn't answer. Every child, however, received a prize – a book, usually on a religious theme,
with a certificate stuck in the inside cover signed by some clergyman we didn't know to say that the book was a prize for superior
answering at an RE examination. By this method, before leaving
primary school every child was the possessor of a Bible and
hymnbook and prayer book.

At these exams there were children from the junior forms of
Tate School, the local Church of Ireland secondary school. One
year during a break, while the pupils were out in the graveyard,
a fight broke out between a sixth class boy from the National
School and a boy from Tate. Like gravediggers, they had thrown
their jackets over two headstones and slugged it out. There were
no punches to the body and no wrestling: the two stood toe to
toe and exchanged vicious blows to the head. It was a sweltering
June day and sweat poured down the face of each as they
ducked and swayed and absorbed blows without flinching. I
had never seen anything like it. The girls had scattered and boys
stood in a circle round the fighters shouting their support for
one or the other. I had no idea what the fight was about but
needless to say I supported the boy from my own school. The
fight went on for a full five minutes and only ended when the
bell went and each boxer took his jacket and lost himself in the
crowd of children pushing towards the door for the second half
of the exam.

In June too the annual sports and party for children was held
in the rectory grounds. Parents helped to organise games for the
little ones and races for the bigger ones. The day ended with a
mothers' race followed by lemonade and buns and tea for the
adults. At the end of the Christmas term there was a Christmas
party in the YMCA with a visit from Santa Claus. A big
Christmas tree stood in one corner of the large hall and held a
present for every child in the parish. After games and tea, most
of the lights were turned off, voices were lowered and the children sat down to wait for Santa. The atmosphere, electric with
anticipation, was shattered by a couple of unmerciful blows on

the door that frightened the living daylights out of some of the little ones who hadn't an idea what was going on. Some of them ran screaming to their mothers while others were rooted to their seats in terror. All eyes were on the door which was opened to admit the bearded red and white figure, bent in two, limping on a blackthorn stick with a sack on his back. He hobbled towards the Christmas tree helped by one of the teachers, and in response to enquiries for Rudolph, or questions about the weather at the North Pole, mumbled inaudibly into his cotton wool beard. He put down his sack, miraculously straightened his back and proceeded to distribute the presents from the tree. The older ones went up quickly to collect their presents but the further down the list he went the more mothers or older brothers or sisters appeared to collect presents for frightened little ones. When the job was done the children gave three cheers for Santa, led by Miss Elgee, then he mumbled his way back to the door, waved his stick in the air, without falling over, and disappeared.

One was only conscious of being Protestant when confronted with something distinctively Catholic. Whereas Church of Ireland clergy wore dark suits and clerical collars similar to Roman Catholic priests, we had no equivalent to Franciscan Friars in their brown habits, bare feet and sandals. In the grounds of the Friary on John Street there was a huge chestnut tree that produced the finest of chestnuts. In school in the autumn the 'countries' would arrive into school with a good supply of chestnuts and, keeping the best for themselves, would give the poorer ones to the 'townies' and then proceed to beat them hollow at conkers. Passing by the Friary after school one day, I saw children busily collecting chestnuts. Only one thing stood between me and some decent conkers with which to challenge the 'countries' – a large friar standing at the gate, arms folded. After much thought and with not a little trepidation, I approached the friar and asked if I might collect some chestnuts. Without moving he nodded his head and in I went. I had this overwhelming feeling of being on 'holy ground' under false pretences, somewhere I shouldn't have been. I began collecting under the tree, fearful that one of the other children might recognise me and challenge me, a Protestant, with taking Catholic chestnuts. I quickly collected the best conkers I could find and left. It was still no contest, however, for the 'countries' who had devised a way of seasoning their chestnuts on the range in the kitchen at home against which the fresh soft conkers from the Friary were no match.

As I grew up I became slowly aware of how Catholics perceived Protestants to be different, mainly from my friend Dick who was a Catholic and went to the Christian Brothers. Dick was slightly older and was a good friend. In fact he was protective of me and in matters of religion he was very matter of fact.

'Protestants don't believe in the Blessed Virgin.'

'Yes, we do,' I said.

'No, you don't,' Dick said with great authority, 'We were told in school.'

'Well, whoever told you is wrong,' I replied remembering the words of the creed we said in church: '… born of the Virgin Mary.'

The big difference was, of course, that we were not going to heaven and children chanting from the far side of the street sometimes reminded us of this:

Proddy, Proddy go to Mass,
Riding on the divil's ass,
When the divil rings the bell
Proddy, Proddy goes to hell.

We were also reminded of our small numbers:

Proddy, Proddy on the wall,
Half a loaf would feed ye all.

We had no such clever jingles to reply, and all we could do was lick the air and chant: 'Cat lick, cat lick, I'd hate to be a cat lick,' and run as fast as we could since there were always more of them than there were of us.

My life did not revolve entirely around the Church of Ireland parish and school and Church of Ireland friends. Especially in the long summer holidays I knocked around with Dick and some of his friends from the Christian Brothers school. They would sometimes talk about school from which I gleaned that theirs was a tougher regime than that of Miss Sherwood.

On fine summer days we would swim at least twice a day at the 'Bathing Place' at the far side of the railway tracks just before the New Bridge, which was still called just that despite the fact that it was ancient and had barrels with planks the full length of it to slow down the traffic in case the bridge fell into the river.

One morning, drying ourselves after a swim, plans were laid to rob an orchard. It was taken for granted that I was included and I sang dumb even when I discovered that the orchard was at the rectory. This was not a sectarian decision. The rectory was targeted simply because it was easily accessible from the lower road and the orchard was only partly visible from the house. I had never robbed an orchard before but I hadn't the courage to chicken out. As we approached the end wall I volunteered to be the one to stay on the wall and keep watch. If Canon Hazley or his wife came down from the house at least I wouldn't be caught red handed. The orchard was bounded by a stone wall and merged into the garden at the top end. The other three climbed over the wall while I lay on top, partly hidden by ivy and some overhanging branches. I had a view of the whole orchard and into the garden, and into other gardens on either side.

Suddenly I heard the three on the ground running for the wall and then the sound of Canon Hazley's voice. I pressed myself as flat as I could into the ivy on top of the wall and could see Canon Hazley in shirtsleeves and clerical collar followed by his wife. I lay perfectly still, frozen to the spot. My heart thumped in my chest until I thought it would burst. Then the voice familiar from quite another context: 'The brats, if only they'd come and ask I'd give them apples when they're ripe.'

They turned and walked back up the orchard. My heart slowed as I saw them disappear into the garden. Despite my discomfort I had no intention of moving until they were inside the house. Then I heard the muffled voices of the others on the outside of the wall. I lowered myself down and my legs were so weak I could barely stand.

'That was close,' said one of them.

'It was even closer for me,' I said.

'Aren't you a Prod? Sure he'd have let you off.'

'Shut up,' said Dick, pushing the boy to the ground and walking away.

There was in my mind as a child an association between the Roman Catholic religion and ghosts. I had never heard talk of the supernatural or of ghosts either in my own home, in school or in church, apart, I suppose, from in the Bible. But certainly not in the contemporary world. I had, however, a confusion of impressions of miraculous appearances of the Blessed Virgin, ghosts and ghost stories. It was as though Protestants had no concept of the supernatural while Roman Catholics were quite comfortable with it.

I had heard of Lourdes and Knock that didn't figure in my religion but seemed to have great importance for the boys who told me about them. These same boys featured one night shortly after the mother of one of my friends had been killed in a tragic accident. We were together in a house a few doors away on a black dark winter's night when two of the boys came in from the back garden, pale faced and frightened, swearing they had seen Mrs Pierce's ghost moving up and down across the back gardens. Everyone, except me, blessed themselves as the boys poured out their story corroborating each other's account, and at every new piece of frightening information they all blessed themselves again. I was scared stiff. Then two other boys decided they were going out to see for themselves. Before they went they blessed themselves. They came back and had seen the ghost too, and they all blessed themselves again. The mother of the house seemed to me to take the story every bit as seriously as the children, which was what frightened me most. Soon after, I left and ran all the way home where my parents told me without equivocation: 'There are no such things as ghosts.'

When my parents went out at night, which wasn't often, Mrs Scanlon, the mother of one of the men who worked for my father, came in to babysit. She was a widow in her sixties, on the low side of medium height, and plump. She wore her grey hair in a plait, wound round in a bun at the back of her head. Her complexion was sallow and her face deeply lined and when she smiled, despite being dressed completely in black, the world lit up. We loved her.

At first we would play rummy for matchsticks, but before bed there always had to be a ghost story. The atmosphere of our big old house with disused attic and basement was ideal for ghost stories on dark winter nights. However, for Mrs Scanlon this wasn't enough. She wouldn't start until the light was turned off, and the dancing flame of the open fire cast eerie shadows in the darkened room. She made up the stories herself and would brook no interruption while her story unfolded. The spectres weren't just in the story, they were in the very room in the darkness behind our backs, so that we would not even turn round until the story was over and the light turned on. It wasn't uncommon, if things got to too great a pitch, for my sister to make a dash for the light switch. If we were too frightened Mrs Scanlon would shrug it off: 'Sure isn't it only an old story.' For an adult maybe it was 'just an old story', but to a child it was something more.

These ghost stories weren't in the same category as the 'real' ghost in the back garden or the accounts of the appearance of the Virgin, but they showed an interest in matters spectral that wasn't in my own upbringing.

CHAPTER THREE

The King's Hospital

When I was in sixth class in Patrick's Square my parents had to make a decision about my secondary education. The options were the two Catholic boys' secondary schools in Wexford, St Peter's College, run by diocesan priests, and the Christian Brothers, or a Protestant boarding school. Tate School had recently closed down. At that time it was almost universal that Irish parents would want their children educated in schools of their own religious tradition if at all possible and so my sister had been sent as a boarder to Mercers School in Dublin and the decision was made that I was destined for Dublin, too, to The King's Hospital.

A number of Englishmen came to Wexford after the war to technical and managerial jobs in one or other of the local factories. These were mostly Protestant families whose children went to our school but whose parents did not attend church. When these children came to secondary level their parents sent them to one of the Catholic schools in the town, while indigenous Protestant families sent their children to Protestant boarding schools. The English families, although sharing the religious background of one of them, did not belong to either of the local tribes. In one case, enthusiastic nuns in one of the convent schools caused a bit of a stir in the Church of Ireland community by angling to convert one of these English girls to Catholicism.

Mary had prepared me as thoroughly as she could for The King's Hospital entrance exam early in the summer.

'Patrick,' (she always used my full name when she was cross) 'Patrick,' she shouted for the whole room to hear, 'while you're gazing out the window sucking your pen the other boys will be answering questions and gaining marks.'

The King's Hospital was founded in 1669 with a charter of Charles II. It's full title was: 'The Hospital and Free School of King Charles II, Dublin.' Aldermen of the city of Dublin dominated its Board of Governors, while for a period Jonathan Swift was also a governor, and the pupils were the sons and grandsons of freemen of the city. The term 'hospital' in the title denoted a charitable institution for the maintenance and education of the young. When I went there in 1951 the student body was still exclusively Church of Ireland.

At the entrance exam there were boys from all over the country: self-confident Dublin boys and nut brown farmers' sons, writing for all they were worth to gain admission to this venerable institution, with the cheapest boarding fees in Dublin. Lunch was in the large dining-hall where over the mantelpiece there was a carved-wood royal coat of arms and a portrait of Charles II.

The day after the entrance exam, back in school, Mary asked to see the papers. She declared that they were fair and asked me how I had answered some of the questions. As far as I was concerned the exam was over and I didn't want to think any more about it, but kudos for a teacher rides on how well their pupils do and such enquiries are not always without a teacher's self interest.

The school holidays stretched ahead and going away to school was a hundred years away. There was swimming, tennis at the boat club and cricket. However, the nine pence pocket money left after the deduction of church collection was not adequate for normal schoolboy needs. One week this nine pence was not enough to buy a ball I wanted badly in Mrs Bridges' shop. Mrs Bridges, who would have known me, kindly said I could pay the remaining two pence next week. On learning this in the middle of lunch my father stood up and marched me the length of the North Main Street to return the ball until I could afford to pay for it. This particular lesson failed, as in adult life I had mortgages, overdrafts and even bought a Hoover on the ESB bill by instalments. Fund raising was necessary to augment meagre pocket money. This found a friend and me selling old newspapers to the furniture factory and picking blackberries for the local agent of some jam factory, and even digging up an old range in the back garden to sell to Jamsie Meyler's scrapyard in Selskar. The cinema, cigarettes, backing the odd horse under the tutelage of one of Hadden's apprentices, and anything else that grabbed the free spirit of boys during the long summer holidays, all came at a price.

September came, and back to the real world. The outfit list signalled a strange new world – hockey stick, rugby knickers, tuck box and school cap. My father's big leather suitcase was pressed into service and filled with items ticked off the list. My apprehension began to build as the day approached, not helped by my sister's accounts of boarding school life. From being a big fish in a small and familiar pool, I was about to become a small fish in a big and unknown pool.

The day arrived and the journey with parents to Dublin and The King's Hospital, now the Incorporated Law Society in Blackhall Place. The front hall was a chaotic confusion of boys and parents, trunks and cases. Safely delivered, equipped and funded, my parents left me in this ancient building to continue my education.

In due course the unfamiliar became routine. A life lived by bells, books, classes and games, sleeping in a spartan dormitory of forty boys. The main thing to be learned was how to keep out of trouble, not easy when you didn't know the 'rules', but you learned them quickly enough. Ration books handed in for frugal portions of butter and sugar if there was any left at all by the time the plate or dish arrived at your end of the table. One square meal a day: dinner. The others: porridge, bread and tea; and tea and bread.

The headmaster was the Reverend J. J. Butler, a Church of Ireland clergyman who determined the whole atmosphere of the school. He was the son of an RIC officer at a time when for police families the priorities of life were discipline and educ-ation. A clergyman he might have been but he was also a mar-tinet – an autocrat and a dictator. He was a big man with a shock

of grey wavy hair, who filled a passageway as he progressed
from one place to another, so that boys stood back against the
wall when they saw him coming. If a boy had reason to speak to
him, which wasn't often, the Head kept walking and the suppli-
ant had to keep up with him and hope he got an answer before
he disappeared up the stairs to his apartments.

Butler had a ferocious temper which he didn't lose often, but
when he did he would beat a boy severely with his hands or a
strap in such a way that if a teacher were to do it today he would
be up in court for assault and battery. This seemed to be the
norm in schools of the time and perhaps it is unfair to judge then
by the standards of now. What clerical headmasters of those days
did, however, about the biblical injunction to unconditional, for-
giving and self-giving love I don't know. Maybe they thought it
was necessary to beat children in order to love them. I'm sure
they justified it by the advice of Solomon in the Old Testament:
'Spare the rod and spoil the child', especially when they were
other people's children, although parents did it too. But then we
all quote the Bible to reinforce our own prejudices. Fear was a
large part of Butler's, what we would call today, management
style.

Apart from teaching Latin to senior forms, Butler's contacts
with boys were mainly when the whole school was assembled at
prep and at meals. He came into the big schoolroom at the end of
first prep every night and made announcements. These included
forthcoming events, alterations to routine, lost property and
general warnings and sometimes threats to the school at large.
These he followed with prayers read from the Prayer Book.

What is to be said in his favour? He was a man of his time. He
was a headmaster of his time. He was fair in the terms of the
strict regime he ran. He ran a school on a shoestring making a
good secondary education available to boys whose families
might not otherwise have been able to afford it. Above all, he
was genuinely concerned for boys when they left school and
was often instrumental in getting them placed in jobs when jobs
were not easily available. He had a love of classical music and,

through extra curricular recitals from his own record collection, introduced boys to good music.

His assistant masters were a mixed bunch. The unmarried ones lived in and the married ones lived out. Their job was to teach and to implement the Head's regime. The Irish master had the unenviable job of trying to teach boys, very many of whom were antipathetic to the subject, enough Irish to pass the Intermediate and Leaving Certificate exams. He did this by long lists of vocabulary and by grammar and consequently boys who came from good National Schools lost very quickly any Irish conversation they had. He reinforced the abhorrence of the language for some boys by giving hefty impositions for words or points of grammar missed. There's always the exception: one boy went on to do Irish at university and subsequently taught the subject and published in Irish. The science master, on the other hand, taught by sharing his enthusiasm and inspired many boys who pursued the subject in one or other of its branches at university.

The most civilised and cultured of the masters taught English. He performed at every possible opportunity. Much of what he did wasn't on the curriculum at all, and he was oblivious to what sense the class made of his performances, turning English literature into a complete mystery for many. He would arrive in the classroom head down, gown flying, bang his chalk box and books down on the desk and start to read from some poem or novel that took his fancy. One of his favourites was *The Rubaiyat*. When he had read a few verses he would close the book with a flourish and say: 'From the Rubaiyat of the Omar Khayyam of Naishapur in the province of Khorassan who lived in the twelfth century, now what must we do today?' all in one breath. He didn't encourage comments or questions at the time, but he was more than willing to talk about it after class or to lend the text to anyone who showed an interest.

Sexual awakening and the harmless experimentation that accompanies it were the usual part and parcel of boys' boarding school life. There was, however, a more sinister side to this department. One assistant master, a Church of Ireland clergy-man, used to rub himself in class on a boy's hand on the edge of a desk and was known to have boys to his room for sexual favours. One former pupil told me recently that this master brought him one night to the theatre and during the perform-ance tried to grope him. He became furious when the boy suc-cessfully forestalled him. This kind of thing was well known to most of the boys and was taken as 'normal' and joked about in the way that schoolboys do. I have no idea how this master selected his targets or whether he damaged these boys. I think the boys he was involved with were few, but he was rumoured to augment their pocket money. I have no doubt that other staff members knew about this too, but did nothing about it. It is, however, clear that this sort of thing is not exclusive to one de-nomination or another.

In King's Hospital sport was king, and if a pupil was good at games he had a particular status with both masters and boys alike. Boys who were non-sporting, many of whom were good at other things, were somehow inferior beings. Honours ties were awarded to members of senior teams and a boy who got to sixth form without an honours tie was an oddity, no matter how good he might have been academically or perhaps at music. Compulsory games were rugby and hockey, the latter of which I believe was played only by boys in Protestant schools, and cricket and athletics in summer. We also played tennis and handball, in which the Head took a particular interest. It developed, no doubt, during his childhood in Cork and Kerry. The handball alley adjoined Collins Barracks next door and, despite the height of the wall, handballers spent a fair portion of their time shout-ing 'Ball please' in the hope that a passing soldier would return the ball.

The ethos of the school, of course, was mainstream Church of Ireland but not self-consciously so. It was also generally speak-ing nationalist. Perhaps some of the boys from border counties were not from nationalist families but there was no sense of any-one being unionist. One boy, a rabid republican, read aloud Dan

Breen's *My Fight for Irish Freedom* by instalments in the dormitory at night before 'lights out' and he got a hearing. His aunt, a primary school teacher, offered him a substantial sum in cash if he came first in his class in Irish. His enthusiasm for Irish revolutionary history was, however, greater than his competence in the language and the prize remained unclaimed.

Religion was an integral part of school life. Before class every morning there was a short service in the school chapel, conducted by the headmaster with lessons read by a rota of senior boys. On Sundays there was an early Communion, before breakfast, for boys who chose to go. Sunday mid-morning the whole school filed into chapel, masters wearing gowns and academic hoods, for a sung service, including an anthem performed by the choir which was excellently trained by the school organist. When this service was Holy Communion, the Head celebrated and he also preached, but the attention span of boys wasn't always what it might have been. On one famous occasion, processing out of chapel behind the choir, carrying the Communion vessels, he encountered a boy whom he had seen misbehaving during the service. He handed the vessels to a choir member, gave the boy a few belts, took back the vessels and continued his procession to intone the prayer of dismissal for the choir.

The Head also prepared boys when they came to the age for confirmation. The only thing I can remember of my confirmation classes, perhaps unfairly, was the Head's veiled and circumlocutory reference to the evil of masturbation without using the word. At the end of confirmation classes he gave candidates a printed sheet of set prayers that I preserved and found useful at a stage later on in my life.

The first class on three mornings a week for all forms was RK – Religious Knowledge. The course was the *Church of Ireland General Synod Board of Education Syllabus for Secondary Schools*. The subjects were Bible, catechism and Irish church history and there was an exam at the end of the year. Despite the exam in the summer term it is generally true to say that boys did not treat the subject with the same seriousness as other subjects. Subjects that related to one's mortal career took precedence over a subject that might affect one's immortality. I suspect that teachers did not give the subject the same weight either. Outsiders, perhaps local clergy, invigilated the exam itself and serious cogging was not unknown.

A boys' boarding school in the early fifties was a rough enough place to be and, since a fellow had no choice but to be there, he learned to cope with it and get on. It is often said that such and such a school turns out fine young people. I don't believe this is true. Parents and early upbringing determine largely how children turn out. Schools can have only a marginal influence one way or the other, if any. The King's Hospital in those days had a tradition going back almost three hundred years, during which little had changed in educating the sons of Church of Ireland families. Today The King's Hospital, now in Palmerstown, has become one of the most expensive schools in Dublin, educating the sons and daughters of mainly well-off families of different denominations.

Academically I did as little work in school as was necessary to stay out of trouble. Nobody explained to me the purpose of working hard at school, and if they had it would probably not have made any difference. School work was just something that had to be got through. There seemed to be an element of competition amongst those who did well and I by nature was not competitive. I was content to survive. I was keen on sports, but even there I was not competitive enough to be more than average.

I had no sense that doing well at school would lead to a better kind of job after school, such as the bank or insurance, or even to university from where one was bound in those days to get a decent job of one kind or another. I had no sense at all of 'after school', no sense of purpose. Not only had I no idea what I wanted to be, I had no concept of becoming anything, and I certainly had no sense of wanting to 'do well' or make money. I lived a day at a time with an eye on weekends and holidays, and that was as far as it went. Most teaching was geared towards exams, which was natural, but with few exceptions little effort was put into making subjects interesting, capturing the imagination of boys to motivate them to take a real interest.

By doing enough to keep in the middle of the class, school reports were never too bad. They were never very good either. They were peppered with the usual comments that school teachers use: 'Could do better.' 'Not using his full potential.' 'Does not concentrate.' 'Exam result disappointing.' My parents must have been tolerant or even liberal as I don't remember having to explain myself at home.

Towards the end of my third year in King's Hospital my father died. One year later I sat the Intermediate Certificate and passed it without distinction. By this time I had convinced my mother, who had moved by now to Dublin, that if I did not return to school after the Inter, not only would she not have school fees to pay, but I would get a job and earn some money. I have no idea who she consulted, but I'm sure she consulted somebody, and since I wasn't making much impression on academia it was agreed I should leave school and find, as they say, gainful employment. A poor Inter qualified me for very little and in 1955 jobs were scarce, but a secret weapon was employed on my behalf.

I am not and never have been a member of the Masonic Order, and I know very little about Masonry, other than what Masons will tell you, which is that it is not a secret organisation, but an organisation with secrets. As I understand it, these secrets are to do with Masons being able to identify each other if they have a mind to, without the rest of us ordinary mortals knowing a thing about it. They also have rituals they perform in secret, that, contrary to popular belief, have nothing to do with goats. Masons in Ireland will be very quick to tell you that Masonry in Britain and Ireland, though sharing with continental Masonry a common ancestry in the medieval craft guilds, is none the less a different kettle of fish.

Masonry is an all-male activity, members of which must believe in a supreme being. Tradition has it that a woman hid in a longcase clock during a lodge meeting, heard more than she should have and therefore had to be inducted as a mason, the one and only female member ever. Women, however, are allowed to help to serve and wash up at annual dinners that are of course not lodge meetings. Roman Catholics are forbidden by their church from becoming Masons, presumably on the grounds that Masons may get up to things that may be in conflict with their Roman Catholic Church membership and over which the church has no control.

In addition to all of this, The Masonic Order is a charitable organisation, concerned to dispense charity primarily to the wives and children of its deceased members, especially for education. Up to relatively recently, it owned and ran schools exclusively for the children of deceased Masons – the Masonic Schools. At a time when there was no free secondary education in this country and social services were not as they are now, this was an inducement, or at least a bonus to membership. Furthermore, unofficially Masons would be well disposed to help the widows and orphans of deceased members in whatever way they could, especially in the matter of employment.

My father had been a Mason, primarily I believe for its charitable benefits, and so when I left school, through my mother's contacts with Masons I quickly found a job.

CHAPTER FOUR

All work and no play ...

I started work in G. A. Brittain & Co Ltd, Portobello Bridge on 11 July 1955 at the age of fifteen, a man of the world! These were the days of buttons in the flies of men's trousers and misfares boxes on the platforms of Dublin buses; when women stood discreetly into doorways to fix suspenders to make sure their stockings stayed up, and when acknowledgments from the Revenue Commissioners for conscience money appeared on the back page of *The Irish Times*; the days before zips and tights, when people paid their dues and when scandals were scandals and not everyday occurrences.

These were also the days of Catholic and Protestant firms. G. A. Brittain & Co Ltd was definitely a Protestant firm, while Carrolls of Dundalk, the manufacturers of Sweet Afton cigarettes, had the reputation of employing only Catholics. In Brittains the Protestant tag referred to management and a bias in favour of Protestants on the office staff. Had they wanted to, there weren't enough Protestants around to staff a firm that size exclusively with Protestants. Considerably less than half the office staff were Catholic, but the workers on the assembly line were exclusively so. Brittains had another reputation – that of being the lousiest payers in Dublin. I started work at £2.2.6d.per week – in today's money £2.12½p. After about six months the boss called me in, told me he was pleased with my work and gave me an increase of 12½p. Even with the raise I still had a long way to go before I would pay income tax.

Under the protectionist economy of the time, assembled motor cars could not be imported into Ireland. They had to be imported CKD – Completely Knocked Down and assembled here. Brittains of Portobello Bridge was one such assembly line, assembling Morris and Riley cars. These were the early days of the Morris Minor and business was brisk. The last man on the assembly line had a little pot of red paint and a fine brush with which he painted, free hand, a line on the body of each car on a raised strip under the windows on both sides, perhaps the last hang-over from the decoration of carriages from which motor cars had evolved .

I started as a clerk in the spare parts department, working with a storeman in charge of stock control. I knew nothing about cars and when I started I wouldn't have known a back axle from a cylinder head gasket, but I soon learned and spent my time counting anything from nuts and bolts, half shafts, piston rings, cylinder head gaskets to bonnets and mudwings, and entering the numbers on sheets to go to the Hollerith Room to be punched onto cards to be processed by the Hollerith machine, a mechanical precursor of the computer. After a matter of weeks in the store, I was transferred upstairs to sit at a desk with boxes of Hollerith cards on either side of me at the end of a chute, checking invoices from the spares department to ensure items invoiced were in stock. I was bored stiff, but the crack in the office was good.

There was Mr Carlson, cashier, Mr Hare and Mr Gibson, clerks, Miss Wolfe and Miss McAlpine, typists, and myself. Christian names were not used at work. Mr Hare was an *agent provocateur* who led Mr Gibson up all kinds of verbal alleys. The game was to provoke him to declaim, in mid-Atlantic accent, on any topic of the day. It wasn't difficult as he was glad to give a definitive opinion on anything. Miss Wolfe chipped in from time to time with feathery comments, while Miss Mc Alpine never volunteered anything unless she was asked a direct question, when she smiled a most appealing smile, blushed to the roots of her being and said the minimum required to forestall further questions. I listened and enjoyed the crack. Mr Carlson, who cycled his bicycle all over Europe on his summer holidays, sat with his back to the rest of us and grinned. When consulted, he would

give a serious and considered opinion, not unwilling but, I suspect, unable to relax enough to enter into the spirit of the hu-
mourous agenda. However, when things had gone on long
enough or when things might have got out of hand he would
gently but firmly call the office to order. These occasional
episodes served to relieve the monotony and make the working
day tolerable.

When I worked in Brittains first I stayed in the YMCA Hostel
a few doors up Rathmines Road. There was full board accommodation for about sixteen young Protestant men, mainly from
the country. The charge was modest, but not so modest that on
my meagre wage I could afford it without a subsidy from home.
There were advantages to living there: I had no bus fares to
work and I didn't have to get up too early. On more than one occasion when I overslept I nipped into work, suit over pyjamas,
to clock in and went back to wash and dress.

In Dublin the YMCA was an organisation that promoted a
particular kind of puritan evangelical religion and the Hostel
was designed to be a safe Christian environment in the big bad
city for young men away from home. However, the lodgers
were there mainly for the cheap accommodation and they were
well aware of the city, its dangers and its attractions, and some
of them frequented its cinemas, dance halls and public houses,
none of which would have met with the approval of the Hostel
management. All that was required of residents was to be of
good behaviour, pay their rent and turn up for breakfast on
Sunday morning.

Unlike weekdays, when people got their breakfast when they
arrived in the dining room, Sunday morning breakfast was at
8.30am for everyone and all residents were expected to be there.
The Warden turned up in Sunday suit with Bible under his arm.
Some of the residents arrived washed and spruced ready to go
to church after breakfast. Others, suffering the effects of
Saturday night, dishevelled and half asleep, had jacket and
trousers over pyjamas ready to go back to bed. At the end of
breakfast the Warden would stand up and read a passage of

scripture and expound it with evangelical fervour and challenge all present to give their lives to the Lord. He was a big soft countryman from the North of Ireland with a great sadness about him at the lack of response to his message. He was kindly towards his charges and wanted them to be saved, as he was sure he was, in order to secure for themselves a place in heaven.

The routine was the same every Sunday morning. A few of the young men were of the same theological bent as the Warden but most were not. Some were suffering from at best a late night and at worst an enormous hangover. Some of the older ones were inured to the ritual and resented both the compulsion and this brand of religion being imposed on them, and during the testimony humorous and sometimes profane comments issued, *sotto voce*, and sometimes not so *sotto*, from their end of the room.

That first summer out of school I played cricket with YMCA Cricket Club, solely because a cousin of mine was particularly friendly with a member who played there and introduced me. During one of the first matches I played I was sitting waiting to bat when two players sitting beside me, very friendly to a new member, steered the conversation from the vagaries of the weather and the state of the wicket to the evils of the world and the state of my soul. I was not in the slightest interested in thinking about the state of my soul, much less willing to discuss it with two strangers. I parried their comments and questions and tried to bring the conversation back to the game. Eventually they invited me to a meeting that evening, but I lied politely that I was already going out. For the rest of the season I steered clear of the two 'evangelists', and with reckless disregard for the state of my immortal soul I joined Leinster Cricket Club the following season, by which time I had also left the YMCA Hostel in Rathmines. I was living with my mother in Monkstown, where the digs were free, the home comforts excellent and where I was looked after as only a widowed mother can look after her only son, and Sunday morning was a pretty conventional Church of Ireland service in the local parish church.

I had been working in Brittains something over a year when

one morning I was called to the phone. It was the unmistakeable voice of Butler, the Head. I froze.

'Is that you, Semple?'

'Yes, sir.'

'I 've arranged an interview with an Insurance Company for you, will you go?'

'Yes, sir, thank you.'

'Have you got a pen?'

I took down the particulars.

'Good luck,' he said and was gone. I was stunned.

I arranged a day's holiday and went for the interview to The Scottish Provident Institution, a Scottish Life Company in College Green. The manager, a pint sized man with a pronounced Scottish accent, sat behind a large desk.

'You only have the Intermediate Certificate. Entry is normally a Leaving Certificate.' I sang dumb.

'However, Mr Butler recommends you and I trust his judgment. If I were to employ you, would you sit the Insurance Institute Preliminary Examination which would enable you to take the rest of the Institute Exams?'

Now I knew insurance companies' pay scale from friends, which meant that if I got this job I would earn approximately twice what I earned in Brittains, and if he had asked me would I climb Nelson's Pillar on the outside in my underpants, I'd have said 'yes'.

Ten days later I received a letter from the Scot offering me the job. I was on top of the world and set for a career in that most secure, permanent and pensionable business of insurance. The world was at my feet but before I took a kick at it my mother reminded me that I must write to the Head and tell him I got the job and thank him. This I willingly did and when he died some years later I went to his funeral.

I handed in my notice in Brittains and on my last Friday I was presented with a silver cigarette case engraved with my initials by the general office staff. The male clerks arranged a pub crawl that night that ended at a 'bona fide' in Brittas, 'The Blue

Gardenia'. On Saturday morning Brittains got their pound of flesh when I had to turn up to check spare parts invoices for the last time, with a little man with a hammer beating hell out of the inside of my head.

My new job in College Green was a short walk from Tara Street Station. Every morning the same train from Seapoint, the same people waiting on the same spot where their carriage door opened, make for the same seats, some to sit on their own and others to join those already there from further up the line. The same ones every morning were last minute, breathless, scramble for any door and sometimes too late and miss the train. Seated, passengers read morning papers or talk, or just look out at sea or backs of houses, each one in their own way coming to terms with another working day. At Westland Row and Tara Street some jockey for position and push on, others walk slowly on the edges refusing to be rushed. All funnel past the checker, down the ramp and disperse throughout the city to observe more rituals in their day's work, and in due course return for evening trains.

As jobs went in Ireland of the 1950s, insurance was second only to the bank. With exams and patience and loyalty to the company, it was a good job with prospects. Trade Unions were 'infra dig' and the harmless and genteelly named 'Guild of Insurance Officials' was ignored by the company. The insurance world was better known for those who left it than those who stayed. They left to broadcast, act, entertain and follow dreams. Boredom drove many to take risks to make something more of life than salary, perks and pension.

The company I worked for was a small Scottish Life company where thrift, economy and industry were the bywords. Light weight envelopes were used to save postage and stationery costs, and stationery was carefully monitored to avoid waste. There were eleven employees: eight inside, two inspectors and the boss. The boss and the inside men were Protestant, the inspectors were Catholic and the women were some of each, making it exactly 50/50; one version of fair play when the proportions in the population were 95/5!

I started doing that essential, but most menial of all tasks – the post book, and every other menial job around the office including answering the phone. In those days you just answered the phone with the name of the company, not today's 'So-and-so speaking. How may I help you?' In fact my mother taught me an important lesson about answering the phone. Not just about answering the phone, but about myself when answering the phone and about men in general.

The gas cooker was malfunctioning so my mother phoned the gas company to come to fix it. They didn't come, so she phoned again. They still didn't come so she phoned a third time and still they didn't turn up. She asked me to phone them, saying: 'They ignore a woman, but they'll listen to a man.' I phoned and they were out immediately. I then realised that when I answered the phone in work, if it were a man calling I hopped to it and took more notice than if it were a woman. My mother, a widow, was left to fend for herself in what she frequently referred to as 'a man's world'. She discovered the hard way that business-wise some men ignored or took advantage of women. On more than one occasion I heard her say, 'I hate men.' She was a feminist in the 1950s, long before it became a movement, and she convinced me from her experience that she was right.

The office was more relaxed, to say the least, when the boss was out than when he was there. He was an intimidating little man. He made up in bluster what he lacked in stature. He had the 'cashier', a gentle man by nature, distracted trying to keep the staff compliant to his will. For some reason, however, the boss himself seemed to pick on one particular typist and sometimes had her in tears. It was entirely necessary, in order to keep a sense of proportion in such an atmosphere, to create some light relief from time to time. This the other junior clerk and myself did. However, when the cashier judged that things had gone far enough, he would call one or other of us down the back to be admonished. Offices that haven't got a natural one among their staff should employ a modern equivalent of the court jester to keep their employees amused in order to make the tedium of office work tolerable and consequently more productive.

The work was routine and boring. During the morning I looked forward to lunch time and during the afternoon I looked forward to five o'clock. It was a job, and jobs weren't easy to come by in Ireland of the 1950s. The few bob at the end of the month came in handy to fund the important things in life – cricket in the summer and rugby in the winter, and particularly the social life that went with them.

Observatory Lane was a narrow entrance off the busiest part of Rathmines Road. The lane was named after Thomas Grubb (1800-1878), an optician who became a world-renowned optical engineer, who lived there. He designed telescopic equipment for observatories in Britain and Ireland and worked with Lord Rosse on the great telescope at Birr. This narrow lane, wide enough to allow passage of only a single car, opened out to reveal a great circular field that was Leinster Cricket ground. Over to the right was a Victorian pavilion and on the left some tennis courts, another pavilion and a bowling green. The magical atmosphere of the place has been destroyed in recent times by the opening up of the lane and the replacement of the cricket pavilion by a bland modern one.

Leinster Cricket Club was, to say the least, a sociable place. It took its cricket seriously and it took its sociability seriously too. Like many sports clubs, and unlike YMCA, it had a bar and, needless to say, it was around the bar that the social life of the club revolved.

It is hard to convince the uninitiated that cricket is one of the most fascinating games there is. To the outsider it may look boring or even ridiculous, but to the player it is full of the most absorbing subtleties of weather, the state of the pitch and the pace and spin of a ball through the air and off the ground. There was no greater pleasure than fielding when that character of Leinster cricket, Paddy Boland, was bowling and under his breath giving his own running commentary on every ball he bowled. When he had beaten the batsman all ends up and the ball had whistled a hair's breadth over the bails, as he walked back to his mark polishing the ball on his groin: 'A little slower and a little more air

and be the jizzes I'll get him this time.' If you love cricket you'll
know what I'm talking about and if you don't, put it down as
just another of life's mysteries. For the enthusiast there is no better way to spend a warm summer's day than playing cricket and
afterwards retiring to the bar.

The bar in Leinster was 'men only' which, at the risk of
sounding patronising to women, was no harm given some of the
rugby club type songs that were sung there late on Saturday
nights. Some of these songs were harmless and very funny but
some of them stretched the bounds of decency and the words of
some of the parodies come to mind even today when I hear the
tunes of the originals. If, however, there were enough female
camp followers in the clubroom outside, who earlier in the day
had prepared the tea and had done the usual kind of women's
work, the party might move out there. In the bar sometime after
closing time the barman pulled down the shutter and served
drinks from the door at the side as long as there were customers.
Occasionally a pair of Gardaí (male only in those days) from
Rathmines station turned up. Having signalled their arrival in
advance they found everything in order, including some bottles
of stout and two clean glasses on the table in the outer room that
they could not ignore. They removed their hats, addressed the
bottles of stout and everything returned to normal in the bar.

There are cricket club members who suffer from an obsession
with the game long after their playing days are over. They watch
cricket at every opportunity and like nothing more than to talk
about the minutiae of the game, and to discuss in detail players
and matches of the past, with statistics to support the stories
they tell, for cricket lends itself to statistics. Dessie, a retired
bank official, a bachelor, was one of these. He stood at the end of
the bar counter on Saturday nights and engaged in conversation
anyone who would listen as they came up to order their rounds.
When there was no one at the counter he talked to himself, and
when the shutter eventually came down he talked to it. Dessie
always demurred when called on to sing but when pressed further he launched into a fine tenor rendition of 'Gortnamona',

and sang it through to the very end – a performance that raised the tone of the average evening's songs. The best performances of the evening however always came from 'The Mohawk' and his brother, two elderly gentlemen who performed old music hall songs, always ending with 'Robinson Crusoe' with its chorus, 'So where did Robinson Crusoe go with Friday on Saturday night?'

As far as religion was concerned, Leinster was well mixed, Protestant, Catholic and Jew, at least one. When a team was away on tour conscientious attention to religious duty on Sunday mornings was notably better among Catholics than Protestants. No matter how bad Saturday night had been, and it usually was, the Catholics to a man got up for Mass, while the Protestants fell into three groups: those who went to church because they wanted to, those who went to church in order not to let the Protestant side down, and those who went for the Sunday papers.

The group of friends that I belonged to was evenly mixed religiously and the subject of religion sometimes came up late at night. The Protestants were less clear about their own religion than the Catholics were about theirs. Protestants were clear about what they didn't believe and were less sure about what they did believe but were happy to discuss it anyway. The Catholics thought they knew what the Protestants didn't believe. They did, however, know precisely what they believed themselves and could state it clearly, but they seemed reluctant to develop it or discuss it further.

The truth of the matter was, of course, that both groups were almost certainly not stating what they believed but what their churches taught. They were, in fact, affirming their respective tribal allegiance, and had they not both been indoctrinated in their own tribal teaching and were prepared to work things out for themselves, individuals on both sides might have come to different conclusions. Both sides were prejudiced and for their own security found it necessary to defend their own tribe. In this kind of discussion there is a lot of talking and very little listening, and what listening there is is only with the outer ear, long enough only until it is time for the listener to start talking. In those days these discussions tended to concentrate on differences, while in these ecumenical days they are much more likely to concentrate on what is believed in common. If things ever became a bit serious there was always someone to interject a bit of humour so that nobody was offended by these late night, lounge bar 'theological' discussions. The group seemed to carry within it an awareness of difference but a determination not to let it matter.

The other thing that many people are brought up not to discuss in public, politics, was to my memory never discussed. However, late in the evening someone was likely to strike up 'Kevin Barry' and the whole company joined in, and after it without a break we continued straight into 'The Sash'. On these occasions one was never sung without the other. It was in the bar of Leinster Cricket Club that I learned the words of both these songs. 'The Sash' was not in the tradition of Protestantism in which I or most southern Protestants were brought up and if Catholics could render it as lustily as they did, I saw no reason why I shouldn't sing it too, and for the same reason: to balance the tribal account.

Old Wesley Rugby Club was traditionally Protestant. That is not why I joined it but because some of my friends played there. I thought I ought to play some winter sport in order to keep fit. I had played rugby at school without any distinction but in Old Wesley I trained conscientiously during the week and was a three quarter of one kind or the other on either the 3rd As or 3rd Bs, the lowest teams in the club. Why these teams were not called the 4th and 5th teams I could never understand. I was young for club rugby, lightly built and neither wiry nor strong, but enjoyed the game up to a point. However, I discovered that in rugby, as in so many things, one's mind and attitude are more important than one's physique. I often felt fearful seeing the size of some of the players of a visiting team arriving for a match. Big bruisers of men twice my size and weight who if they were to hit me hard in a tackle, I wouldn't get up for a week. Most of these man mountains were forwards, where at my level of rugby brute force was everything and, as a wing or a centre, my association with them during a match was minimal. Anyhow I learned survival techniques such as that in tackling, no matter how big most fellows were, they were the same size around the ankles. However if all came to all I employed the live coward/dead hero principle. It's strange but somehow once I was togged out, on the field and the game got going and the blood was up, for some reason these bruisers didn't seem as threatening as they did fully dressed.

There was something about the hot shower after the match and the anticipation of the few pints to come that made it all worthwhile. You might be badly bruised or have pulled or twisted something in the game but in the shower afterwards you felt good. Playing away in Clontarf was even better, where you could soak with ten or fifteen other players in the giant tub filled with hot water, a luxurious end to the afternoon no matter what way the match had gone. Showered and dressed you felt you had earned the pints and the Saturday night ahead whatever it held.

Old Wesley still had associations with Wesley College and the Methodist ethos, and consequently did not have a bar, since Methodism is hot on temperance if not on total abstinence. Longs of Donnybrook, however, filled the needs of the drinking membership of the club's four or five rugby teams returning from around the city. In the tiny lounge pints were consumed to replace lost liquid as games were analysed and as tactics, scores, referees and anything else you like to think of to do with rugby were expertly discussed. The squeeze of bodies and kit bags, the talk, the laughter and the repartee, the shouting of orders and the passing of dripping pints over heads was bedlam for an hour or more. Slowly the shandy drinkers and the married men began to drift away, leaving a hard core transmuting pints until the hunger began to bite.

Three or four of us were nearly always amongst the last to

leave. We made for the Coffee Inn in Anne Street where they served a moderately priced spaghetti bolognese of large propor- tion, and from there to the bar in The Wicklow, where stout was tolerated, but only in bottles.

The bar of the Wicklow Hotel in Wicklow Street was at the other end of the spectrum from the lounge in Longs. It was car- peted and had a high polished-wood counter. There were stools for the counter and upholstered chairs for the glass topped ta- bles. Behind the bar were mirrors that reflected the inverted bot- tles of spirits with optics, and bottles of exotic drinks on shelves that nobody ever seemed to drink.

The Wicklow on a Saturday night was a rugby haunt with what seemed to be a preponderance of Protestants, from Old Wesley and some from Wanderers and Trinity. Some of the Old Wesley members that had left Longs early came with wives or girlfriends, and late on there might be an influx of Wanderers alikadoos from their clubhouse in South Frederick Street. Sometimes amongst the Wanderers group was 'Snipe', a Church of Ireland country rector observing rugby's Saturday night ritual after his day in Dublin to watch a match. During the evening, strains of Gilbert and Sullivan on violin, and appetising smells wafted into the crowded bar from the dining-room down the hall, and by closing time we had laid plans for the rest of the night and into the small hours of Sunday morning. Despite everything, if we ended up going home after the Wicklow the night was a failure, though this seldom happened. There was usually a party, a dance or an excursion to a 'bona fide' for the next instalment of the evening.

There were two kinds of party: ones you were invited to, and ones you had to crash. Crashing parties in flats was quite accept- able but in people's homes it was different, especially if there were parents around, not that many young people would hold a party unless their parents were away. Crashing wasn't quite crashing either, as word was passed round earlier in the evening by someone who knew someone who was invited, and we wouldn't crash without some kind of a contact, no matter how tenuous. Anyhow, as long as you arrived with your brown paper bag to contribute to the stock of booze, you had a good chance of not being thrown out.

The second option was a dance. Tennis, hockey or rugby clubs, particularly Palmerston and Wanderers, were the usual haunts. Whichever of these, the routine was the same. Unattached women sat or stood around the sides of the dance floor appearing to chat nonchalantly while the men, most of whom arrived after a night's drinking, eyed and assessed them like cattle at a fair. When the music started the men crossed the floor to invite the woman of their choice to dance. What factors went towards influencing that choice is only to be wondered at. I find it difficult at this distance to remember! I suppose a fellow might see a girl he knew already and liked and ask her. Or a fellow might see a girl he knew and for one reason or another definitely did not want to ask her. She might be a friend of his sister or he might have asked her at a dance before and she walked all over his feet. If a fellow was five feet four he would be unlikely to ask a girl six feet tall or if he was six feet two he would be unlikely to ask a girl of five feet nothing.

Of women that he has never seen before, what makes a man ask one woman to dance rather than another? It is a mysterious something, an indefinable mystical motivation, the earliest stirrings of something more exciting and profound, by which nature eventually seduces us to conspire together, and over which we have little or no control, in order to procreate the species. We are the playthings of nature. Some people call it lust. Take your pick. Dances were organised on the face of it to make money, but were clearly occasions for whatever you want to call it, so it is no wonder they were equally abhorred by puritan evangelical Protestant preachers and conservative Roman Catholic bishops, who proscribed dances in their diocese during Lent, and one can't help feeling would have done so altogether if they thought they could have got away with it. The more certain one is that there is life after death, the more likely one is in this life to see anything to do with pleasure as sin. Church of Ireland clergy in general didn't seem to have an opinion one way or the other, other than to run what they called parish 'hops' in the hope that their young parishioners wouldn't marry Roman Catholics.

Altogether apart from the fears of preachers and bishops, how poor unfortunate women could stand on one side of a hall and be looked at or even leered at by men from the other side, who would breathe stout all over them for the duration of three dances, I do not know. It was unheard of for a woman to refuse a man to dance. It would humiliate or almost emasculate a man if a woman refused his invitation to dance, and in those days it didn't happen, but it was not uncommon, as soon as the music started, to see a woman working her way to the back of the crowd and as far as the cloakroom if necessary, to avoid a hopeful making a beeline across the floor to ask her. Too late to turn back he then had to ask casually someone nearby in order to save face. How women felt that weren't asked at all I can't begin to think. There was, of course, the occasional 'ladies' choice', a token acknowledgement of their disadvantage, and the 'Paul Jones' when neither the lady or the gentleman had choice.

If dancing were your hobby, you would have had to arrive at these dances early. By the time we arrived they were packed and for quick dances men had to steer their partners, as best they could, around the crowded floor. For the slow lie-in dances everyone more or less stood and moved around the floor with the crowd, all the time trying to make conversation about anything except the reason both were there.

Failing a party or a dance, the 'bona fide' was the third possibility after The Wicklow. The licensing laws of the time acknowledged that travelling was thirsty work, and so allowed 'bona fide' travellers, should they happen upon a hostelry on their journey, to drink after hours. To qualify as a 'bona fide' traveller one had to be more than five miles from where one had lodged the previous night if that was within a County Borough, and three miles if one had lodged the previous night in other than a County Borough. In order to facilitate travellers who might suffer from thirst as they passed by, the city was ringed with well known 'bona fide' pubs. The Blue Gardenia of my leaving-Brittains night out was one such, but the one we happened most often to be passing late on a Saturday night when we felt the thirst rearing up again on our way home from Wicklow Street to Kenilworth Park, Rathgar Road and Monkstown, was The Widow Smith's in Stepaside. There we would meet other thirsty travellers on their way home, and despite the fatigue of our journey we would force ourselves to be sociable until the small hours.

Whether parties, dances or 'bona fides', Saturday nights/ Sunday mornings went on long after the last bus. There were fewer cars on the road then and travelling around and especially getting home was always a problem. None of us was in the league that owned a car nor did any of us have access to one, but the most venerable member of our group had a scooter, and sometimes he had to ferry us around. There were no breathalysers; the test of sobriety then was to walk a straight line in the Garda station. Provided a driver didn't hit someone, consuming large quantities of alcohol and driving didn't seem to be a problem. It is clear that people thought little of driving with drink unless they were really drunk and often even then people drove and got away with it. For us cadging or hitching lifts or long walks home were an unfortunate feature of early Sunday morning, or perhaps dossing down for the night in a friend's flat. On more than one occasion I met my mother at the church gate in Monkstown for church and breathed stale stout down the neck of the people sitting in the pew in front for the duration of the service.

CHAPTER FIVE

TCD

I was 19 and starting to learn something of the ways of the world. Two Edith Piaf songs come to mind: *'Non, je ne regrette rien.'* No, I regret nothing, and 'Those were the days my friend, We thought they'd never end,' but of course they did. Bill qualified and went away, Duffy had other fish to fry, as he usually had, Dick took up golf and I became aware of something else.

What is a vocation and how do you know you have one? It's a bit like the physicist and electricity – he knows a lot about how it behaves but can't say what it is. It's like an electric shock – you know if you've had one but all you can do is try to describe the effect it had on you. For me it was unmistakeable. However, for me, unlike an electric shock, it happened slowly. It was a process not an event. An overwhelming sense of unworthiness and of dependence; of being acceptable and being accepted despite everything. A sense of the need to give back something to God, not for his sake but for my own, in order to feel good or right with myself. I believed that the only way I would feel at peace was to be ordained. Why this was so I do not know, it just was. Sometimes people try to avoid it or deny it but, as in Francis Thompson's *Hound of Heaven*, it pursues you, it torments you, it doesn't leave you alone until you acknowledge it. All other possibilities seem to close off leaving it the only possible option that can give you peace. It is an intense feeling that permeates your whole being but that somehow comes from outside, from beyond, from God.

In practical terms, as vocation grew I missed the odd Saturday night, which was most unusual. I never asked them, but I'm sure the lads thought I was sick. Without telling anyone I began saying prayers again and reading the Bible. Attending church took on a new meaning, and in due course I had to talk to someone about it, and the obvious person was the local rector.

In this I could not have been luckier; the local rector was the Reverend Billy Wynne. Around this time he was in the process of founding 'The Samaritans' in Ireland, fighting a battle against the Catholic Church authorities who believed Samaritans wasn't necessary in Ireland as the church could cope with its own depressed, destitute and distressed members. Billy Wynne was a man uncorrupted by piety and he had a great love for people. He talked about the church as 'not a museum for saints but a school for sinners.' A verse he used to quote:

And the devil did grin

For his favourite sin,

The pride that apes humility.

I went to see him once a week for a number of weeks and told him everything. One of the first things he told me was to be sure not to lose touch with my friends. I might be about to travel a particular route but my friends would help me to keep my feet on the ground. I had no intention of losing touch with them though things were changing for all of us.

After a couple of months Billy Wynne agreed that I should explore the possibility of ordination further and he put me in touch with the Warden of the Divinity Hostel and Secretary of CACTM, The Central Advisory Council for Training for Ministry, which had only recently been established by the Church of Ireland bishops to oversee the selection of candidates for training for ordination. Up to this time a candidate for ordination had to convince an individual bishop that he had a vocation and get his agreement to ordain him after he had done the required academic study and passed the exams.

The rector made an appointment for me with Canon John Simpson Brown at the Divinity Hostel, Mountjoy Square, where ordinands lodged while studying at Trinity. John Brown and Billy Wynne were as different as chalk and cheese. John Brown was a bachelor, a former schoolmaster, not that I could ever envisage

him in a school classroom. I arrived at the Hostel and was
shown into his study that had been the drawing room of the
Mountjoy Square Georgian house. It was four o'clock on a winter's afternoon and the Warden sat behind a large desk opposite
the door on which were piles of books and files. There was no
light in the room and I could barely see him until he stood up.
He was like a clerical Humpty Dumpty. In appearance only, I
hasten to add – a round head on a round body, thinning grey
hair sleeked down, flushed cheeks and thin lips, and wearing a
dark grey suit and clerical collar. He sat down again and said
nothing. As I began to wonder did he know who I was and why
I was there, he said, barely audibly, 'Mr Wynne has spoken to
me,' followed by another long silence. The conversation staggered on but he certainly wasn't going to put words in my
mouth. I told him I was considering ordination but he made no
comment one way or the other about why or about vocation or
anything to do with it. That which was so important to me at this
time and the reason I was there he made no comment on. He
played his cards so close to his chest that foolishly I might have
made the mistake of thinking he couldn't see them himself. I
was determined not to initiate conversation; for I felt this was a
game of which I didn't know the rules. After another long silence he said:

'Can you matriculate?'

I knew it wasn't to do with sex but I didn't know what it had
to do with.

'I beg your pardon?'

'Have you got Trinity entrance exam or equivalent?'

'No, I only have the Inter and some of the Insurance exams,
but I'm prepared to work for Trinity entrance.'

'I'd like you to write an essay on any topic of your choice, and
send it to me,' which was about the longest sentence he spoke,
and even then he stopped in the middle of it and swallowed.

Then he stood up and brought me to the study door and put
me in the charge of one of the students to look after me for
chapel and supper.

The chapel was a converted room at the back of the house. The service was Evening Prayer with two hymns, conducted by one of the begowned students, and then we went to the dining room for supper. I was brought by my minder to sit beside the Warden who was at the top of one of the tables. This time he was more relaxed and in conversation with the student opposite to me he actually smiled. Again I spoke only when I was spoken to, and even then ventured no strong opinions. After the grace at the end of supper, the Warden said goodbye and my minder showed me out the front door, back to normality. I heaved a sigh of relief to be back on the street, back in the real world with normal things happening around me and I wasn't sure how, if I got that far, I was going to cope with living in that kind of atmosphere.

I wrote the essay and sent it to the Warden. After about six weeks, not having heard from him, I phoned to know if I ought to begin to work for Trinity matriculation exam. John Brown didn't like answering questions and replied to mine by asking another. 'Would you be prepared to go to a selection conference?' I told him I would and next day I got the Trinity entrance exam syllabus and started to study.

Some months later I received word to attend a selection conference at Murlough House, Co Down, an old country house at the disposal of the Church of Ireland for conferences.

At a dress dance in the Gresham Hotel a couple of weeks later, Kevin, who occasionally turned up in Longs on a Saturday afternoon, or whom I met at a party late on a Saturday night, came over to me.

'I hear you're going to CACTM.'

'I am,' I said, surprised he knew.

'I'm going too.'

So we arranged to go together and I was certainly glad of the company entering the unknown.

Kevin was older than I was and since he was a small boy he was determined to be ordained. He was a miller and had recently passed Trinity matriculation exam. CACTM was his last hurdle before starting out on the final lap of achieving his lifetime ambition. He had a healthy disregard for the pomposity of some academics and ecclesiastics. On Professor Hartford, Regius Professor of Divinity making no reference to being long overdue when he arrived for an appointment to interview him, Kevin looked him straight in the eye and said: 'You're late.'

A Church of Ireland CACTM selection conference lasted for three days during which the candidates were interviewed and assessed as to suitability for ordination by a bishop, two clergy and two lay people, under six headings: academic, psychological, social (capacity to work with people), church involvement, spirituality and vocation. As a result of the conference candidates were accepted, deferred or not recommended.

Murlough House was a large country house on the coast of County Down on loan to the Church of Ireland from the Downshire family for most of the year. It was remote and ideal for a conference.

If I was nervous going I was even more nervous when I arrived and met the other ten or twelve candidates, mostly from Northern Ireland, a somewhat different breed of Church of Ireland member from those I was used to. Among them there was a school teacher, a couple of clergy sons who had gone straight from school to university and who always intended entering the family firm and seemed to know it all, and some older men from business. Most of them were heavily involved in their parishes and knew a lot about the church and who was going to get the next vacant bishopric, probably before it was even vacant. I knew the name of only one bishop, the Archbishop of Dublin, and that was because he had preached in Monkstown a few weeks before. It seemed to me that the world outside church and religion barely existed for most of these candidates and if it did exist they didn't talk about it. For me and, as it happened, also for Kevin, the opposite was largely the case: we knew more of the world than the church, so I talked little and listened much to be confirmed in my view that the experience of those that talked most was very different from my own.

There was one older man among the candidates, probably in his forties, who seemed to have the unfortunate knack of getting into problems. He was probably nervous and spilled coffee, got lost and was late for chapel and set his alarm clock for half an hour before we were due to be called. On one morning while trying to turn it off, he knocked it onto the polished wood floor, got out of bed and kicked it under someone else's bed, scrambled to retrieve it and eventually turned it off. After the conference we never saw him again. He was probably advised that his vocation, his unique and distinctive contribution to the life of the Church, would best be served as a layman.

The examiners were pleasant people who did everything they could to put us at our ease. I can only remember one question I was asked by any of them. A layman examiner asked me if I were listening to my favourite radio programme and someone from outside came in what would I do. (In 1961 not everyone had a television.) I said I would turn off the radio, which was the answer I knew he was looking for. He seemed taken aback by the firmness of my answer and wondered, if it were near the end of the programme would I not excuse myself and hear it out, or perhaps it might also be the favourite programme of the visitor and maybe he would like to hear the rest of it. No, I said, I would turn off the radio. I said it definitely as I knew it was the well-bred thing to do and since the examiner was clearly a member of the landed gentry, complete with double barrelled name, I knew he would be impressed.

There was a strong churchy atmosphere at the selection conference that I found suffocating. Just like I was glad to get back out into Mountjoy Square after my appointment with John Brown, I was glad to get back to the real world after the conference, and on the way home glad to see ordinary people going about their normal business, something similar to what a prisoner must feel on release. It didn't daunt or deter me. I felt confident in my vocation, but I hoped I would not be expected to cultivate something of this churchy way of behaving if I were to be the genuine article. For the time being I decided to keep an open mind. After all, they might turn me down.

During this time I was seeing aspects of the Church of Ireland that were new to me. We all like to think that what we believe and feel about things is the norm, but I was learning that, as an Anglican Church, the Church of Ireland carries within it a diversity of theological position and practice. One of the great mysteries of the Christian religion is that Anglicanism, in all its diversity, holds together at all. For the moment I was in suspense, not knowing if I was acceptable as a candidate for ordination or not. I was glad to get home to my own bed, scrambled egg for breakfast and the train to work, though impatient to get on with preparation and training for what I hoped for the future.

In due course the long awaited letter arrived. I had been accepted and the plan for me was a degree at Trinity followed by a Testimonium in Divinity with pastoral and spiritual training at the Divinity Hostel. I was greatly relieved, and with a fierce determination I studied evenings and weekends for Trinity entrance. There was no points system in those days but the university allowed entrance on Leaving Certificate results that of course I didn't have. It had been only a matter of a few years previously that entrance was gained on an honours Intermediate Certificate. At the end of a year's study I passed the entrance exam and finally matriculated. Around this time there was a backlog of older men who felt called to ordination, whose families when they were younger could not afford to send them to Trinity to follow the only route then available for training for ordination in the Church of Ireland, or perhaps they were academically unable to enter. Some of these men were taking a two year Trinity non-graduate course in biblical studies for mature students. At twenty two I wasn't old enough to take this course.

The insurance office I worked in was right opposite the Bank of Ireland at Trinity front gate so I had watched the shenanigans of students over the previous six years, and here I was, becoming one of them. It somehow didn't fit but it was so and I entered in the Michaelmas term, October 1962. There was an interesting mix of men entering Trinity that year intending to be ordained. Some were in their thirties but among them were three sixteen or seventeen-year-olds, sons of rectories, two of whom won entrance sizarships. Academically they were very good but their life experience was, to say the least, limited. In due course one of them became a bishop and another left the ministry and the country under a cloud. As with the selection conference the majority were northerners, unionists to a man, while those of us from the south were nationalists. Tolerance of diversity extended even to politics, but there were arguments that were hot and heavy. There was incredulity on the part of southerners that some of the northerners could hold the views about Catholics and the south that they did, and they, no doubt, were incredulous of the nationalist and ecumenical views of southerners. Nobody that I knew of fell out, but there was constant banter of a half-joke-whole-earnest kind. My group of friends in college, not all Divinity students, were older and had all worked for a number of years since leaving school. All were southerners except one, an exceptional northerner, Fred, who was more tolerant than the rest of us.

At this time Roman Catholics were banned by their church from attending Trinity without dispensation, for fear of the corruption of their faith and morals. When a dispensation was given it was sometimes granted on condition that the student attended lectures only and did not join any of the university clubs or societies. Consequently the university had an unmistakeably Protestant ethos, consistent with the majority of faculty members and students being Protestant, and the Divinity School within the university being Anglican and training exclusively Church of Ireland ordinands.

I enjoyed student life compared to the strict routine of office life. It was a great liberation. Apart from perhaps two or three lectures a day, the freedom to come and go as one pleased, to sit and drink coffee and indulge in the kind of conversations students have – talking without listening, statements rather than questions, much of the abstract but little of the concrete, and having ready answers to the great imponderables, believing that truth is easily known. Most divinity students were members of the College Theological Society with rooms in East Chapel where arguments of great intensity reflected the theological and political diversity amongst the aspiring clergy. I found little support for my own sceptical approach to matters of belief. If there is a prototype for all of us in the gospels, mine was Thomas. I marvelled at the uncritical acceptance of many of my colleagues and in some cases their absolute certainty.

At first I was a conscientious student. I attended every lecture and worked hard until I got the measure of things and then relaxed and enjoyed the life of college. I felt the privilege of having the opportunity of going to university and was determined to make the most of it. For degree I studied philosophy, history and Greek. Philosophy out of curiosity, history out of interest and Greek because I was told it would be useful in New Testament studies later on. In theory it was a good thing to be able to read the New Testament in the original but I'm not convinced that it was worth the effort and it is doubtful if any subsequent parishioner will have benefited from my being able to do so. Within a few years of being ordained I had forgotten most of it.

There were grants from the Church of Ireland for impoverished Divinity students but these barely covered the essentials, so in the long vacations it was necessary to work to accumulate some money to keep the wolf from the door during term. The first Christmas I sorted mail in Blackrock Post Office and at the end of the first year I worked in Manchester, in the fierce heat of a factory, extruding rubber surrounds for car doors and windows, and living in a flat with two others from Dublin. This work was part of a course for Divinity students to learn what it was like to work on the factory floor, and a couple of evenings a week under the tutelage of a neighbouring rector to reflect on the theological and pastoral issues. The rector became ill so this bit never happened, leaving us free to become involved in the local parish where the rector was an Irishman and one of the churchwardens was pilfering money from the Sunday collections.

In the second long vacation I went with a friend to Canada and worked on a building site as an inspector, where I was initiated into the mysteries of structure checks, piezometer readings and slump cone tests, none of which would be of much use to me in the average Church of Ireland parish, but the pay was good and dealing with the Italian workers advanced my general education. The Italians were affable, voluble and not entirely reliable, and when challenged they waved their arms in the air and broke into Italian, the only word of which I could understand was the 'f' word.

When we finished work on the building site, with two friends from Trinity we travelled the circumference of North America with rambler tickets on Greyhound buses. We got off the buses in cities and at places of interest by day and slept on the buses by night to save accommodation costs, but every third or so night we were so exhausted we stayed in a hostel or cheap hotel. I wasn't brought up to read my Bible every night but one of my travelling companions was. He was a medical student, son of a well known evangelical clergyman and I admired the way, even on the bus, last thing at night before settling down he would read his daily scripture portion. He didn't drink but wasn't offended when we had a beer to quench the thirst. His eyes were out on sticks, however, when in a bar in San Francisco a topless waitress appeared to take our order. We were all, to say the least, surprised but when we ordered two beers and a coke she advised us that the way prices were scaled we would need to be drinking all night to get value for money and suggested a bar down the street. She was topless but she was kind.

At the end of third year at Trinity another friend and I went to Rotterdam to work for the summer at the Mission to Seamen, known to seafarers as the Flying Angel. During the day we visited, by launch, ships moored in the harbour and returned again in the evening to bring seamen ashore for the night, either to the Mission clubhouse or to go down town. We provided the service, they made the choice. The clubhouse had a bar that served beer only, with table tennis and billiards and on some nights there was a film or a dance. The women who came to dance were friends of the Mission, known as 'Harbour Lights' – officially or in jest I never discovered. At the end of the night there was a short service of compline in the chapel to which a few of the sea-men came. Talking to seamen was a revelation. It's a way of life into which most land-bound people have little or no insight. There are men at sea who have remarkable stories to tell.

No matter how quiet or reticent seamen are, they are usually ready to talk about where they come from and who is at home for them, usually wife and children whom they haven't seen in some cases for as long as six months. Some of them talk easily and tell their story, and others are silent and brood.

One night the crew of a Northern Ireland ship spent the evening at the Mission. This was 1965. Two of them, one a Catholic and one a Protestant, best friends at sea, told us how when they went ashore in Belfast they went their separate ways, one to the Falls and the other to the Shankill, and didn't see each other again until their next trip. Later that night outside the Mission, as we were about to go down to the launch to bring men back to their ships, a fight broke out. The two friends from the Falls and the Shankill were kicking the daylights out of an English seaman who had been foolish enough to make a derog-atory remark about the Irish.

For the last two years before ordination, students were obliged to live in the Divinity Hostel, now in Churchtown, during term time, with its daily routine of chapel services. At the Hostel there were lectures for the wide variety of non-graduate ordinands who did all their training there: a miller, insurance and bank clerks, a chicken sexer, an accountant, a civil servant, a sheet metal worker and those straight from school and university. Among them there was a range of theological position, from fundamentalists believing in the literal inerrancy of scripture, to evangelicals who lay special stress on conversion and a personal relationship with Christ, to broad church – interpreting church formularies in a broad and liberal sense – and a few 'spikes', high churchmen, who stress Anglicanism's continuity with

Catholic Christianity and the early church and the place of ritual in worship. All these, contained within the spectrum of the Anglican position of the Church of Ireland, lived cheek by jowl, studying together, worshipping together and arguing the theological toss till the cows came home.

In Bible lectures, some students fresh from evangelical parishes, and often with recent conversion experiences, were prepared to stand up to contradict the lecturer because his biblical criticism did not square with the student's belief in the literal verbal inspiration of scripture. The hope was that by the end of his training students of this kind would have a broader view of scripture – a hope not always realised, especially when the student came from a parish where the rector was of like mind and advised him to listen to all the lecturer had to say, give it back to him in the exams, and then forget it.

'Birds of a feather flock together', and this was so at the Hostel, but meal times, especially dinner in the evening, which was obligatory, was the time when students mixed and sparks, political or theological, sometimes flew. The former 'B' Special from mid-Ulster defending that force to a southern nationalist who had never been across the border, or the fundamentalist arguing that if God wanted to make a whale that could swallow the whole Hostel, let alone Jonah, he could. It was not unknown for a couple of *agents provocateurs* to mark a target for an entertaining dinner.

Some evangelicals had prayer groups that met in their rooms and prayed for some of the rest of us, that we would be converted and become 'real' Christians. In other words, that we would have the same kind of conversion experience that they had had and hold the same view of atonement that they did, and be steeped in the Blood of the Lamb as they were. We are all affirmed and reassured by people who are of like mind, but to say that fellow ordinands were not proper Christians because their experience was different from their own, in my view, showed a deep insecurity, while on the face of it communicating an unshakeable confidence. Some of the discussions became heated. It was bad enough to grow up with Roman Catholics telling you you were going to hell, but when some of your own crowd told you the same it was a bit much.

Some students from the north, where of course most Church of Ireland members live, resented having to come to the south to train for ordination. They felt aliens in a foreign land and took no interest in the south, scuttling back over the border at every opportunity. One of these northern students admitted openly he was in the south under protest, but some years later took a parish in Co Mayo. He either changed his view or he was on a mission. There was on the whole, however, a truce between the parties in the common pursuit of passing exams and fulfilling requirements for ordination.

This was the time of the Second Vatican Council when Catholic seminaries were beginning to make contact with Protestant theological colleges for ecumenical exchanges. Since we were the only Protestant theological college in the south of Ireland we were inundated with invitations and, for practical reasons, had to limit the number we accepted. Some of our early contacts were with the Dominicans in Tallaght, Maynooth, the Jesuits at Milltown Park and the Kiltegan Fathers in Co Wicklow.

At first the contacts were purely social, sometimes a sports fixture. The first one I went to was a rugby match against the Dominicans in Tallaght which was hard fought but nobody took a poke at anyone else. At the tea after the match the Dominican staff member welcoming us referred to the result: a draw, 3 all. 'One try each and no conversions!' Thirty three years later a Dominican friend I worked with in hospital chaplaincy remembered the occasion well, and the thing that he confessed he couldn't get his head around at the time was one of our students telling him he had to leave promptly after the match as he had a date.

There were a couple of Church of Ireland ordinands who would have nothing at all to do with these events; they would have put their heads into a lion's mouth rather than enter a

Catholic seminary. I never knew for certain but I'm sure there were a few Catholic seminarians with corresponding views. We all have our bigots.

When it was discovered that neither side had horns or cloven feet, some of these ecumenical events took the form of discussions under the watchful eye of staff members on both sides. At Maynooth I read a paper on the theme of a Protestant approach to ecumenism, when I used the opportunity to raise the issue of *Ne Temere*. In the ensuing debate a couple of people on both sides became a little heated but the chairman, Fr Kevin McNamara, later Archbishop of Dublin, gently and skilfully defused the situation.

We in turn welcomed Catholic seminarians to the Hostel and appointed a student to be responsible for these exchanges. Myths about each other were exploded and friendships were made among students across the denominational boundaries that in some cases have lasted ever since. A student at Maynooth from Co Galway confessed to me that I was the first Protestant he had ever spoken to. We became good friends and saw each other regularly later on in Belfast when I was curate there while he was at Queens. Nothing but good came from these occasions and my abiding memory of them is of the warmth of welcome and genuine interest shown on our visits to Catholic seminaries.

During my last long vacation in college Hilary and I were married, so for my last year in college I was a kept man. Hilary taught, and what is more we lived apart in term time, she in a flat in Sandycove and I in the Divinity Hostel. Even today the time has not come, but I hope it soon will, when the Church of Ireland will, like some Anglican colleges in England, provide married student accommodation on campus for ordinands.

In Anglicanism bishops don't have the same degree of authority as Roman Catholic bishops. At ordination the newly ordained priest promises to obey his or her bishop's '… godly admonitions' and submit to his '… godly judgments'. I suppose in theory a priest does not have to obey an ungodly admonition or judgment of a bishop, but then what Anglican bishop would ever issue an ungodly admonition or make an ungodly judgment?

So when ordinands come towards the time of ordination they are not directed to their first curacies by their bishops. These days a complicated system is put in place to give rectors, who have been allocated a new curate, and ordinands some freedom of choice as to who will get whom and who will go where. The college sends CVs of prospective new curates to lucky rectors and the rectors send their parish profiles to the college for ordinands. Both rectors and curates will often have strong preferences. An evangelical rector will want an evangelical curate and a broad church rector will probably want a broad church curate and so on. Most northern ordinands will want to go to a parish in the north and some southerners will want to stay south. The occasional northerner will stay south and many southerners will want go north to gain experience of part of the church with which they are not familiar.

In 1967, the year I was ordained, the system was less open and transparent. John Brown, Warden of the Hostel, was a wise and wily old bird. He knew the rectors and parishes of the Church of Ireland like the back of his hand, directing suitable students to meet suitable rectors and much of the time he was right first time. He advised me, as a southerner, that I should serve my first curacy in the north and arranged an interview for me with Alec Douglas, the rector of St John's Orangefield, Castlereagh Road, East Belfast. Alec, a southerner himself, from Co Meath, was a kind and affable man of broad church bent who asked me a few questions, showed me around the parish and offered me the job. I had a few more months to final exams and then Hilary and I were bound for Belfast.

CHAPTER SIX

Ordination

In the week before ordination ordinands for the Dioceses of Down and Connor went on retreat to Murlough House, where six years previously I had attended the selection conference. An ordination retreat is an opportunity to wind down and relax after the frenetic activity of final exams, outfitting oneself with robes and clerical garb, and a dozen and one other bits and pieces that need to be done in preparation for a change of address and a change of routine from student to clergyman.

The week before I went on retreat I had a letter from Archbishop George Simms, who was my own diocesan bishop in Dublin. I had spoken to him briefly only twice in six years on the subject of my ordination. With his letter was an ordination present, a book entitled *Difficulties for Christian Belief*. He knew more about me than I realised.

George Simms was a scholar whose speciality was the Book of Kells. He charmed audiences with his presentations of its beauties and its mysteries. As a *viva voce* examiner in the Divinity School in Trinity he was reputed to fail the weaker students with the same charming smile that he passed the good ones. He had a boyish countenance and a somewhat effeminate manner, but his wife described him as a mailed fist in a velvet glove. He was, as a countryman might say, 'as cute as a bag of foxes'. He had an amazing capacity to remember names, faces and people's concerns, and wrote kind letters to people on the occasion of significant events in their lives. He was a fluent Irish speaker, as were two of his successors as Archbishop of Dublin, McAdoo and Caird. When he was translated to Armagh in the early days of the troubles in Northern Ireland, he was deeply suspect to extreme and even moderate unionists, but he won many of them over in time by his genuine concern for people.

The retreat provides the opportunity for quietness, meditation and prayer in preparation for ordination and what lies ahead. The bishops involved appoint a conductor for the retreat, in our case Archdeacon Jenkins of Dublin, known as 'Jenkie,' who helped us to focus our minds, and there was opportunity to talk to him privately. The atmosphere of the retreat was intense. I didn't really know how to use the time to best advantage; nobody during training had taught us to use silence, to meditate, and even to pray was difficult. Part of the time I wondered if I should have been there at all, but reminded myself that if I had been that wide of the mark someone would have drawn my attention to it before now. I assumed the others all found it straightforward and helpful and I don't know if that was the case or not; on reflection probably not. I felt there was an underlying atmosphere of holiness or piety that I had difficulty with as I would not have applied either of those epithets to myself.

I survived the retreat, and the morning of ordination arrived – the day I had worked for for six years. Along with the bishop we travelled in a minibus to Lurgan for the ordination service. It was a stifling hot day and wearing a clerical collar for the first time, it rubbed uncomfortably on my prominent adam's apple. When we arrived at the church we went straight around the side to the vestry to robe. I wondered if my family and friends had arrived, which gave me a sense of what a criminal must feel when brought straight from prison to appear in court.

The large vestry is full of clergy robing from cases of every shape and size. Normally when robing, the black and white of cassock and surplice is relieved by the colour of university graduate hoods, traditionally worn by Anglican clergy as evidence of their academic qualification to expound the Word. On this occasion, ordination deemed a sacrament, and this particular bishop knowing his onions, hoods are not worn and since coloured stoles were still illegal, considered 'Romish', the vestry was a sea of black and white except for the crimson of the bishop's chimere.

Due deference is paid to the bishop, Bishop Frederick Mitchell, known as 'Fenian Fred' by the Northern evangelical clergy because of his high church tendencies. He is helped to robe by his chaplain. As is frequent in the Church of Ireland, the conversation in the vestry ranges between the weather, the traffic, the merits of somebody's new car and the result of the previous day's rugby international. A number of clergy value quietness before a service in order to focus the mind, rather than a babble of trivial talk. Some people, however, when they are nervous become silent while others cannot stop talking. When the time has arrived hush is called and the rector calls on the bishop to invoke God to bestow his blessing on the service ahead.

The Church of Ireland is capable of performing liturgy excellently and this was one of those occasions. The ordination took place in the context of a sung Eucharist and the whole service came together as a fine piece of liturgy, after which the newly ordained went off with their families to celebrate before turning up for duty in their parishes next day.

Ordination was on St Peter's day, 29 June 1967. On 30 June the rector brought me around the parishioners in the city hospitals and on 1 July he went away for his annual holiday, leaving me to get on with it on my own for a month, with the arrangement that in an emergency I would call on the rector of the next door parish.

I had been in Northern Ireland only twice before I went to CACTM. The first time was on a weekend cricket tour to Bangor, Co Down when, due to a problem with the bookings and something of a 'commotion' in the small hours of Sunday morning, I was ejected from the hotel by a distraught manager. I met a very decent young man about my own age walking past the hotel at about three o'clock in the morning and explained my predicament. He brought me home, went upstairs to get a rug and gave me a sofa to sleep on in the sitting-room. About eight o'clock in the morning, before his parents woke, he came downstairs to let me out. This was before the troubles, before drugs when the worst any of us got up to was a few pints and bit of crack. Every time I pass that hotel I remember the incident and the man, who without knowing me from Adam, brought me home in the middle of the night to allow me to sleep on his sofa.

My second time in the north was on a day excursion for the wedding of a friend from the rugby club. He was a southern Presbyterian and his bride a northern Presbyterian and, while welcomed warmly by the bride's family, I have an idea that we his friends were, as southerners, somewhat suspect to some of the other guests. It was the only wedding I had been to at that point where there was no alcohol. Jugs of orange juice, particularly appropriate, were provided on the tables. As a curate in Belfast I discovered that dry weddings in the Protestant north were not uncommon.

The first of these two experiences hardly prepared me for the change that living in the north of Ireland would be. The second gave me a hint. Before ordination, one Sunday Hilary and I had driven to Belfast to do some work at the curate's house and arrived in the city at about six o'clock. There wasn't an hotel or restaurant open to have a meal. It was the days when children's swings were chained up on Sundays and when garages, shops and restaurants were closed to impose on the population at large a puritan Protestant interpretation of the fourth commandment.

I was a Protestant living in a Protestant area of east Belfast, but I was a southerner and a nationalist. Parishioners would know I was from the south, but I certainly did not wear that or my political views on my sleeve. Proportionate to numbers over the years, the south produced more clergy for the Church of Ireland than the north. There was a long tradition of men from the south being ordained for parishes in the north where many of them spent the rest of their lives. There is an appealing honesty about the northern character and when you receive a warm welcome from people, you know it is genuine. Hilary and I were warmly welcomed. Early on, however, little things hinted at difference!

On my first morning I went into the newsagency a few doors

from the parish church to get an *Irish Times*. I might as well have asked for *Pravda*.

'You're the new curate?'

'I am.'

'You're very welcome, but we don't carry that paper here.'

'Perhaps you could order it for me.'

Silence. I waited.

'Perhaps I could, but you'd have to take it every day.'

I agreed and every weekday for the next three years the newsagent, who was a parishioner, all but threw the paper at me every morning, as if he was defiling himself and his business by handling *The Irish Times*.

On the second night in the parish, Hilary and I were upstairs on our knees trying to fit pieces together to make a carpet for our bedroom when there was a ring on the doorbell. I went down. I opened the door to a man standing on the step.

'Are you the new curate?'

'Yes, that's right.'

'Mr Roberts of … is very ill. The doctor has just left. He says he won't see the night out.'

'Are you a relative?'

'No, I'm a neighbour. They couldn't get an answer from the rectory.'

'The rector is on holiday. I'll go down right away. Thank you.'

I closed the door and opened it again. I called to the man by now at the gate.

'Can you give me the name and address again please?'

He did. I went back upstairs to change into clericals and realised my hands were shaking. My training did not prepare me for this. It's the kind of thing your rector is supposed to train you for but he was in a caravan in Co Galway.

I took my prayer book, marked some prayers, and left. After driving around in circles I eventually found the house and rang the bell. A man in his early forties, wearing a polo neck sweater, grey flannels and slippers answered the door. I introduced myself and he put out his hand, thanked me for coming and stood back to let me into the hall.

'I'm Gordon,' he said, 'My father is very ill. Will you come upstairs?'

I followed him upstairs and into the bedroom where a woman, I assumed to be Mrs Roberts, sat at the far side of the double bed holding the hand of her dying husband, who was propped up on a mountain of pillows. His breathing was laboured and irregular. She stood up and I went around the bed and shook hands with her. I conveyed as best I could commiseration and compassion. She smiled a faint smile of acknowledgment and nodded her head in resignation.

'Thank you for coming,' she said.

I stood up to the side of the bed and looked at the man who was tenuously holding on to life. Mrs Roberts said:

'He has been going down steadily and the doctor says it won't be long.'

Gordon stood at the end of the bed staring with incomprehension at his father. I indicated to Mrs Roberts to sit down.

'I'll say some prayers,' I said, and opened the book at the first marker. When I finished, the other two joined in the Lord's Prayer and I said the Grace.

Gordon sat down beside his mother who was again holding her husband's hand. In the silence the focus of all three was on the patient as with each breath he salvaged a few more moments from life. A dozen and one things occurred to me to say, but all were trite and I resisted the temptation to say any of them. From time to time Mrs Roberts moistened her husband's lips with a damp cloth and adjusted the pillows; small things but all that was left to her to do.

After about five minutes one of two neighbours from downstairs came to the door of the room and, in a tone that was perfectly pitched to be both sensitive and matter-of-fact, said to Mrs Roberts:

'Will you come down for a while? There's a cup of tea ready. I'll bring some up to Gordon and the curate.'

Mrs Roberts stood up, introduced me to the neighbour and went downstairs. Gordon sat onto the chair that his mother had

been on and we continued the vigil. The tea arrived which relieved the strain a little and when we had finished Gordon took
the tray out onto the landing and resumed his place beside his
father.

Mr Roberts' breathing was reasonably regular but shallow.
Every now and again, however, he would stop breathing and
when it looked as if he had drawn his last he would start again.
The first time this happened I thought he was gone and a shud-
der went through me. I was now living from one breath to the
next and dreading what to do when his breathing stopped.

After a long silence Gordon turned to me and said earnestly:

'Mr Semple, we're very glad you've come. My mother and I
have never seen anything like this before.'

'Jesus,' I thought to myself, not sure whether I meant it rever-
ently or profanely, 'neither have I.' Not only had I not seen anyone die before, I had never seen anyone dead.

'I'm glad you sent for me,' I said, meaning it and not meaning it, and adding, 'I'm just sorry the rector isn't here,' and
meaning it very much.

We lapsed into silence again and watched closely. The gaps
in breathing became more frequent and the breathing became
shallower. A pattern on these lines seemed established when
without warning the breathing stopped. We both stood up.
Gordon looked at me to do something. I waited a few moments.

'I think that's it,' I said and watched the patient's chest closely
as there had been so many false alarms. Then there was a coarse
noise from Mr Roberts' throat that confirmed for me that he was
dead. Of the two beside the bed it was clear to me that I was the
expert and the one thing I did not want to do was call Gordon's
mother to say her husband was dead and find he had started
breathing again. I remembered from somewhere the mirror test
and turned to the dressing table behind and found a silver-
backed hand mirror. I held it over the face and mouth for ten or
fifteen seconds and looked at it. There wasn't a hint of haw.
Gordon, mesmerised, looked intently into the mirror and then at
me trying to make sense of this strange ritual. To be sure, I repeated
the exercise and again the mirror was clear.

I turned to Gordon: 'I think you'd better tell your mother your father is gone.'

Looking at me intently he said, 'Gone where?'

'To heaven,' I replied, to keep things simple.

Gordon, without a word, left the room and went downstairs. I used the mirror for a third time and satisfied myself beyond doubt that Mr Roberts was dead. I looked at my watch knowing that for some reason people liked to know the time of death. It was twenty minutes to two.

Mrs Roberts, followed by Gordon and a neighbour, came into the room. I took her by the arm as she came along the end of the bed and up the side. She stood and looked at the still figure propped up on the pillows. She seemed to me to be a sensible woman and I knew she would behave with dignity. I wondered what was going on in her mind. She leaned forward, brushed a wisp of hair away and kissed her husband gently on the fore-head.

Feeling I ought to do something religious I said, 'Will we say the Lord's Prayer together?' and started. The others joined in and when we finished the neighbour put her arm around Mrs Roberts' shoulder. 'We'll phone the nurse; she said she'd get here within an hour.'

She led the new widow downstairs. As soon as they left the room, Gordon looked me straight in the eyes and said: 'What do we do now?'

I had already been thinking about that and had a vague idea there were certain things to be done as soon as possible after death, but wasn't sure how to do them.

'The first thing we have to do is lay him down flat.'

I slipped my arm in behind the dead man's shoulders and held him forward enough for Gordon to take out the pillows. I adjusted my arm to support the head and then realised that if I laid him straight down his head would be propped up against the headboard. Gordon stood looking, eager to help.

'Take hold of his ankles and pull him slowly down the bed,' I instructed.

Gordon looked shocked but such was his confidence in me he did exactly as I asked, and I laid the head down flat and, turning down the bedclothes, I put the arms down by the sides.

I knew it was important to do two things as soon as possible: tie up the jaw and close the eyes. I looked on the dressing table for something like a ribbon or a cord but there was nothing. I didn't want to tell Gordon what I was looking for in case he would go and ask his mother. I took out my handkerchief. It was crumpled but clean. Gordon watched. I folded it diagonally, put it under the chin of the corpse, pulled it tight and there was barely enough to tie a knot at the top of the head. I instructed Gordon to push the jaw firmly up while I struggled to make the knot and after several attempts I succeeded in making one just about strong enough to hold the jaw in place.

The eyes were half closed so I took some coins from my pocket and selected a half crown and a two-shilling piece. In harder times I knew it was two pennies were used but I felt the heavier coins were more likely to do the job. With Gordon looking over my shoulder transfixed, I closed the eyelids and put a coin on each. I pulled up the top sheet and covered the body and couldn't help feeling that for two fellows who had 'never seen anything like this before' we hadn't done badly.

We went downstairs and had tea. We made preliminary funeral arrangements and I left. I arrived home exhausted, going over in my mind the events of the previous hours. When I turned out the light, images of the night's events coursed through my mind. I tried to think of something else, something pleasant or happy but I couldn't. I was haunted by images of the dead man. I turned on the light and tried to read. I couldn't concentrate; the images kept coming back even with the light on. Eventually I fell asleep and had a nightmare that I was in a crowded room with a corpse laid out and I noticed the corpse moving but did not pretend I had seen it. I woke and became obsessed with a combination of the events of the evening and the macabre nightmare.

Eventually I fell asleep and woke early. I had had about two hours sleep. After breakfast I phoned the next-door rector to get his help with arranging the funeral. At about midday I called to the house. The nurse had been and had done the necessary.

We were sitting by the fire in the sitting-room when Gordon came in. He greeted me and said: 'Come upstairs and see him now.'

It was the last place on earth I wanted to go but I couldn't refuse. I followed Gordon into the room, which had been spring-cleaned. The body was covered up to the chin with a single sheet and the mouth and eyes were closed. I struggled to say something suitable and we went downstairs again. I confirmed arrangements with Mrs Roberts and as I left she handed me my handkerchief and the two coins.

I got through the funeral the following day with the help of the neighbouring rector and, by the time the whole thing was over, I was ready for a holiday. My life as a clergyman had begun; I had been thrown in at the deep end and to this day I am whisked back to the night Gordon and I watched his father die by a certain scent of air freshener that had been used in that room.

CHAPTER SEVEN

Belfast

The parish was on Castlereagh Road on the south-east side of Belfast. It had been formed a generation or two before when families were re-housed there from terraced kitchen houses, mainly on the Lower Newtownards Road, where many of the residents had worked in the Protestant-dominated shipyards. By now this area of the parish was peopled mainly by shopkeepers, policemen and tradesmen. In the more recent housing estate of the Braniel, at the top end of the parish, there were more people from the inner city. Many of them still worked in the shipyards and were generally considered socially a step down on the residents of the older end of the parish where the church was. In the Braniel, a hall was used on Sundays for services so that parishioners from there did not have to travel all the way down to church at St John's. This led to a certain amount of two pence-halfpenny looking down on two pence within the parish. There was a third sub area, the Clonduff Estate, also relatively recent, where there was much unemployment and all of the social problems that went with it.

Coming from the south where Protestants were scattered about fairly evenly, except around Bandon where it is said that even the pigs are Protestant, it was strange to live and work where the population was almost entirely Protestant. During three years in the north I had contact with only one Roman Catholic that I knew of, and that was by chance. In the south Protestants were more likely to be respectably middle class; a smaller number were working class, poor or unemployed, and this was not the case in my new parish. Protestants in the north, I soon discovered, were in fact a different breed from Protestants in the south. They were more direct and slower to warm to you. There was something honourable in their directness. You were in no doubt where you stood with them, and when they did accept you they were good and loyal friends. Unlike most southerners they were, however, largely anti-Catholic.

Protestants and Catholics lived in their own areas and didn't have contact, and St John's was clearly a Protestant area. There was no ecumenism. Approaching my first Week of Prayer for Christian Unity in 1968, I asked the rector what we did to mark it. 'Nothing,' he replied.

It was implied that the people wouldn't like it, so nothing happened. Where it was needed most, it didn't happen at all. I suggested that at least we might invite the local Presbyterian, Methodist and Roman Catholic clergy to coffee. The rector told me that if I wanted to have them to my house that was OK by him. I phoned the Parish Priest of the nearest Catholic parish, St Bernadette's, and left a message on his answer machine to say what I had in mind and asking him to phone me back. He didn't. I phoned again and he still didn't phone me back, so I left it there since an ecumenical gathering in the circumstances without the Catholic priest wouldn't have much meaning.

The rector was a kind man and treated me as an adult, unlike some rectors who treated their curates as boys, giving them little responsibility and making them account in the smallest detail for the use of their time. We met every Tuesday morning for a staff meeting when the rector shared out the duties for the week: who would conduct and preach at the services, and the visiting of parishioners in hospital, and sick and infirm parishioners at home.

I found preaching stressful. I realised early on that writing out a sermon and reading it, or even trying to 'preach' from a text, wasn't really working for me, so after a Sunday or two I began to preach from headings. This was even more stressful as there was the danger of drying up or wandering off, but when it worked there was the sense of having been in touch with the congregation, talking to them, rather than of preaching at them.

Visual aids were the fashion of the time but I found it impossible to use them. One young curate, preaching on the parable of the sower, put a bag of wheat at his feet in the pulpit. When he came to preach, 'A sower went out to sow and as he sowed some seed fell along the path', he took a handful of grain and threw it out over the congregation. This caused some slight amusement and a little embarrassment. 'Other seed fell on rocky ground.' And he threw another handful of wheat over the people. 'Other seed fell upon thorns.' Another scattering of wheat. By this time there was wheat in the men's hair and in the rims of women's hats and by the time he came to the 'good ground' the congregation in the front rows were ready to duck.

The same curate one Sunday morning fell asleep in the prayer desk while his rector was preaching. He woke up in the middle of the sermon, stood up and announced the next hymn. 'I wouldn't mind,' his rector recounted afterwards, 'but he announced the wrong hymn.' It's no joke taking services.

Cards from hospital chaplains around the city arrived in the post on Tuesday mornings in time for the staff meeting. They gave the names of patients with addresses in the parish who had given their religion as Church of Ireland. Some were active parishioners, some were paying-in non-attending parishioners and some had no connection at all and weren't known to the parish. Despite everything, the denominational label is strong when the chips are down. The rector divided the hospitals between us and I started first thing after lunch. At around six o'clock I arrived home like a wet rag and fit for nothing for the rest of the day.

One Tuesday I visited a man, a retired shipyard worker in his late sixties, who had been living up the road from the church for more than twenty years but was not known to the parish. He was a retiring sort of person but I knew he was glad to see me. When I went to see him the following week he had gone home so I called at the end of my hospital round. He was alone in the house; his wife was at work. He told me he had inoperable cancer and had three months to live. I asked him if he wanted to talk about it and he replied calmly:

'Not really. There's nothing I can do about it.'

Every Tuesday I called to see him after my hospital round and stayed for about twenty minutes. Sometimes conversation flowed easily and sometimes up to five minutes would pass without a word between us; he was not a man for talk for the sake of it. We talked about this and that and before I left I always said the Lord's Prayer. On a visit five or six weeks after I first called, at the end of a particularly long silence he suddenly said:

'You're a queer fella.' I smiled and asked him why.

'You're a clergyman and you come here every week and talk about anything and everything and then say a prayer and go. I have fellows coming in here every second night of the week trying to convert me. "Your time is short," they tell me, "isn't it time that you were steeped in the Blood of the Lamb, that you gave your life to the Lord before it's too late?"'

I said nothing. He went on:

'If God is a God at all, won't he know the kind I am and I won't be fooling him with a deathbed conversion. I'll take my chances.'

I smiled and he smiled. In a few minutes I said the Lord's Prayer and left.

I continued to visit him every Tuesday at the same time and in due course I got a message to say he had died. I took his funeral and, although I cannot remember his name, I have never forgotten his honesty and his dignity.

Some parishioners in hospital, no matter how ill, are easy to talk to and appreciative of your visit while others, often not seriously ill, would drain you of your last drop of emotional energy. As I worked through my list it was a great bonus to arrive at a ward and find that the patient had gone home, not out of concern for the patient but it was one less to visit. It's sometimes hard to know how ill patients really are. It doesn't do to ask too much detail of a patient's medical condition. One Tuesday, very tired, my last call was to a woman in a geriatric hospital, Mrs Rochford. I hadn't visited her before and when I arrived she was sitting on the edge of her bed in her dressing gown with a face the length of a wet week. I made the mistake of asking her how she was and she told me. She wasn't well and this was wrong with her and that was wrong and she was going out to the nurse to get some pills. She left me and came back with a glass of water and two aspirin that she took with great groaning. I chatted to her for a while and couldn't lift her spirits. I formed the impression since the nurses weren't taking much notice that she was a bit of a hypochondriac and I made light of her complaining. In due course I said a prayer and left. Half an hour later when I walked in the door at home Hilary said: 'The hospital has just been on. A Mrs Rochford is dead.'

As with any job, you learn as you go along.

In due course the rector left me in charge of the 'chronics' list. That is the list of elderly housebound people to whom I brought Holy Communion once a month. One of them was one of the most marvellous people I have ever met. She was a woman in her eighties whose body was so contorted by arthritis that she had to be propped up in a chair with cushions. She could do nothing for herself. Her daughter-in-law was equally marvellous in the way she looked after her. In addition to the arthritis, Granny McBride had a heart condition and half a dozen other things wrong, but as soon as I walked through the door she smiled a most wonderful smile and thanked me for coming. She would talk away, but never about herself, and if I asked her how she was she would say 'Fine' and brush off the enquiry. After a few visits when I told her that my visits to her did me good, she was genuinely puzzled. In time, if I were down in the dumps I would call on Granny McBride and five minutes with her would lift my spirits.

When priorities had been attended to, routine visiting of parishioners from the parish list was the name of the game. Inclusion on the list did not imply attendance at church. About ten per cent, if that, of those on the list were regular churchgoers or churchgoers at all. Most did however 'pay in' which entitled them to be baptised, married and buried at the parish church – Christians on wheels, hatched, matched and despatched. Parish visiting in theory is pastoral care designed to support people in their worshipping membership of the church. What it was when those visited never went to church and had no intention of doing so I'm not sure, but visit I did and with only a couple of exceptions it was appreciated by churchgoer and non-churchgoer alike.

Many of the non-churchgoing parishioners had long associations with the parish and regaled the new curate with their connections and how they had been married in the church, how their children had been baptised and married there. Above all they recounted the names of former rectors and curates they had had dealings with, and all this was designed to prove that despite not going to church, they were *bona fide* parishioners. It was true that most of them had a genuine affection for the parish and all that that meant. One old man, too old now to go to church, spoke in great detail about all the clergy who had been in the parish from the beginning. He spoke as though he had been responsible for how they had comported themselves in their time, implying that if I needed help I might consult him.

A not uncommon reaction from non-churchgoers was: 'Oh I must get back to church, I haven't been for a while.' This was followed by any one of a dozen excuses ranging from: 'I have a bad back and the seats are too narrow,' to 'I couldn't go when my mother was dying,' and this might have been twenty years before. A few of these people did turn up in church for a Sunday or two after a visit and then disappeared again.

One man opened the door and when he saw the collar, before I could say anything, simply said: 'She isn't in.'

For some men in working class Belfast, church and clergy are for women and children, but not for men. It's as though men work, drink and follow football and other manly pursuits, and women look after the house, the children and religion. In order to salvage something from the call I asked politely when would 'she' be in, and by this time a little boy minus his nappy had arrived on the scene and proceeded to piddle on the doorstep. The father grabbed the child and without answering my question withdrew and closed the door.

There was only one other time that I got no further than the door. A woman answered and I started my spiel: 'I'm the new curate at St John's ...' Interrupting me, she launched into: 'I'm fed up with youse ones from the Church of Ireland. There's only one manister in this country that's preaching the true gospel and that's Dr Paisley,' and she banged the door in my face.

Clergy develop a sixth sense when they approach a house as to whether there is anyone at home or not; they develop the skill of reading the signs. A curate friend rang the doorbell of a house where two elderly ladies lived. He had a sense there was somebody in but there was no reply so he rang again. Still no reply so he waited for a long spell before ringing for the third time. By now he was certain there was someone at home so he stood his ground. In due course the door was opened and one of the ladies welcomed him warmly and brought him into the sitting-room to where her companion was. He sat down on the sofa and chatted away to the two old dears, while behind the cushion at his back he felt something hard. Unobtrusively he slid his hand behind the cushion to discover a bottle and two glasses.

There is abroad among some lay people a view of clergy that puts them in the 'I don't smoke, I don't drink, I don't kiss girls, I don't think' category. People see them as holy and good people who do nothing wrong, never swear, say their prayers, know everything there is to be known about Christianity and have no difficulty believing it all, as though ordination conferred holiness and perfection. This is, of course, far from the truth, as I know in my own case and from observing my colleagues over the years! Clergy are recruited from the ranks of the laity and vocation and ordination are to a function and not to a state of perfection. Every human hope and fear, gift and failing, belief and doubt that are present amongst the laity are present amongst the clergy too. The image of perfection that lay people have of clergy creates a barrier between the two and the dog collar and the dark suit compound the problem. Yes, the dog collar is useful and even necessary in some situations but on balance it is a hindrance to honest communication.

Churchgoing parishioners were particularly pleased when the new curate called. They had a proprietary interest. They had seen you in church and knew a little about you from when the rector announced your appointment. That they were parishioners of the same Church of Ireland parish and unionists to a man and woman was about all they had in common with each other. There were all sorts and conditions of men and women who kept up a normal and respectable front with the new curate at the beginning. In due course you discovered that amongst them were all the personal and family problems that you had ever heard of and some you hadn't. These problems only emerged slowly as you came to know people better or as circumstance forced them upon your notice. Here was the raw material of the job, not to be to them a social worker or personal adviser but to help them put their problems and their lives in general in the context of what they believed and what the church taught. These two, however, often transpired to be radically different things. What most people believed, as far as I could glean, was something to do with being good, not smoking or drinking and not being Roman Catholic. They had little overall understanding of church teaching apart from bits of catechism they remembered from confirmation class.

St John's, in common with most Church of Ireland parishes, had its share of 'organisations'.

The rector's wife presided over The Mothers' Union at the St John's end of the parish and the curate's wife presided over the Ladies Guild at the Braniel end. The curate's wife, however, made it clear that she was involved because she enjoyed it rather than because it was expected. The older breed of clergy wives saw themselves as having certain duties in the parish in support of their husbands, like presiding over the Mothers' Union, and they performed these duties faithfully. In fact some of them, strong women, wielded power in the parish outside their traditional role, especially if their husbands were weak, and sometimes even if they weren't.

Some lay people had strange expectations of the rector's

wife. One clergyman to be interviewed by the lay nominators of a vacant parish was asked to bring his wife along. During the interview she was informed that if her husband were appointed her duties would include cleaning the church. Her husband showed no further interest in the parish.

Clergy wives these days don't necessarily have the same involvement in parishes. Many of them work and haven't got time, and some are prepared to be involved if they want to, but won't be involved if they don't want to. Since the ordination of women, no clear pattern has emerged yet of the role of clergy husbands in Church of Ireland parishes!

The Mothers' Union is the largest Christian women's organisation in the world with members in sixty countries. The aims are to develop prayer and spiritual growth in families by study and reflection on family life and marriage and their place in society, and to take practical action in local communities to improve conditions for families. In practice this normally means meetings with speakers on a variety of topics, and action and fundraising in support of projects in the local community. The Ladies' Guild in the Braniel was a similar but less formal organisation, autonomous within the parish; it was not affiliated to any national or international body. The members claimed that they had much more fun and that they were less stuffy than the Mothers' Union.

In some parishes there is a male counterpart of the MU, The Church of Ireland Men's Society. While most parishes have a Mothers' Union, the Men's Society is a rarer bird. This is perhaps because men perceive religion to be more a matter for women than for men. The Men's Society objective is the spiritual development of its members.

St John's, like many Church of Ireland parishes, had an indoor Bowls Club. It functioned at night during the winter and membership was without fear or favour: men and women could join on equal terms. The women, however, prepared the tea and biscuits. It got people out to mix for a night away from their televisions. A night at bowls was most enjoyable and good fun, but it was also deadly serious. If you happened to arrive after a game had started you dare not breathe until it was over. Some of the members were not churchgoers, but they never missed bowls, which for some of them was more their religion than the real thing. The bowls club, in common with other parish organisations, liked one of the clergy to turn up at the beginning to open the proceedings with prayer. Why a lay member saying the prayer wasn't the real thing I'm not sure. It looks like another example of the myth that ordination conveys a magic or a mystique that makes the prayer more efficacious, or perhaps it is a case of 'why keep a dog and bark yourself?' The club played in a Protestant League which meant there was no danger of members being scratched or even gored when playing a match. If Catholic parishes played bowls in those days, and I had no way of knowing if they did, the same principle would probably have applied.

There were the usual junior organisations, Boy Scouts, Girl Guides and Church Lads Brigade, all designed to inculcate Christian principles into young people through the medium of healthy physical activities. The leaders were admirable in their commitment to the youngsters and in the time and effort they expended in running these organisations.

The Sunday School is an important part of parish life. If the country boys in the National School in Wexford thought Miss Sherwood was a walking 'divil' on the rare occasions when she lost her temper, Miss Kennedy, who ran St John's Sunday School, was a walking 'divil' a lot of the time. Even the rector kept his distance. On the Sunday of one Week of Prayer for Christian Unity I preached a fairly mild sermon saying that the Church of Ireland and the Roman Catholic Church should emphasise what they had in common rather than constantly stressing what divided them. After the service Miss Kennedy exploded into the vestry and with no reference to religion or ecumenism informed me 'You'll never get us into a United Ireland,' and before I had time to respond she exploded out again. To be fair to her the matter was never mentioned afterwards and it did not affect my relationship with her. In fact, a year or so later, when I called during the period when her mother was dying she was most gracious.

Miss Kennedy was a teacher in a local primary school so many of the children had her on weekdays and on Sundays. To say the least, she ran a tight ship and her former pupils would say that by the time they had finished in Sunday School they knew their stuff. They would certainly know it by rote.

The further into middle-age people get, the further out of touch with young people they become. Middle-aged rectors find it difficult, if not impossible, to cope with the problem of 'the youth'. So the first thing rectors are wont to ask their new curate is to do something about it. This was my fate on arrival at St John's. Needless to say not every curate is good with 'the youth' either, but when asked one has no option but to get on with it.

I was lucky. There were three or four keen young people, so we formed a committee and began in a small way. We met on Sunday nights in the parish hall after church for table tennis and coffee and biscuits, said the Lord's Prayer together, and went home. As I write this I realise how harmless it all was. The worst we had to cope with was one or two lads going around the back to smoke cigarettes.

It soon became obvious that if the parish were to provide anything of value for the youngsters, the Youth Club would have to meet more often in premises more suitable than the parish hall. There was plenty of open space behind the church so we set about raising money to try to build some kind of prefabricated building there. On Saturday mornings the youngsters ran a car wash and cleaned up people's gardens. James Young, the well-known Northern Ireland comedian, was a parishioner and when he heard about our efforts volunteered to put on a late night performance of his one-man show for us. Parishioners sold the tickets and, having finished his regular show at 10.15pm or so, he went on at 11.00pm and did it all over again in aid of the Youth Club Building Fund. He did this a couple of times, filling his theatre at the Ulster Hall, and gave us a great financial and psychological boost.

We soon discovered that if the Club were open to allcomers and non-denominational, the Ministry of Education would grant aid 90% of the building, the furnishing and the equipping of it, and the wages of a part-time trained youth worker. This began to make sense. The only problem was whether the Select Vestry would be prepared to allow a non-denominational Youth Club to operate on parish property behind the church. Full marks to the rector, he accepted the idea and was prepared to try to sell it to the Vestry.

The night of the meeting came and the rector and I had both done our homework He told them that they had a duty to support the curate and the young people and, without putting a tooth in it, he made it clear that this would mean that Roman Catholic youngsters would be members. To the surprise of us both there was no opposition and in fact a lot of support and the project went ahead. For £7,000 we built a fine purpose-built timber youth centre, with a large hall for ball games, a kitchen, coffee bar, office and two small meeting rooms. We employed a trained youth leader and had a rota of adult parishioners to turn up on club nights and help with the coffee bar and keep a watching brief.

There were two gangs of youths in the area that were constantly 'at war', one in the Braniel, the other in the Clonduff Estate. When the new Youth Centre was up and running the two gangs made a truce and they all came down to join. In fact the gangs merged; the leader was a 'Prod' from the Braniel and his deputy was a Catholic from Clonduff. When they joined, the numbers in the club more than doubled but some of the respectable middle-class parishioner youngsters left. Things went ahead apace and the programme of the club drew the best from the 'gangsters' who integrated well. In fact the local police told a parishioner that since the Youth Centre opened petty crime in the area dropped by approximately 80%. Some parishioners complained that some parish young people weren't going to the Youth Club, and why should non-parishioners use parish premises and cause parishioners to exclude themselves. The simple answer was that that was the way of the world and the way of a government grant-aided youth club. Furthermore, the non-parishioner youngsters needed a youth club more than the parishioner children did.

The paid leader ran the club well and I dropped in from time to time. The more I got to know the tough guys and their 'molls' the more I liked them. Beneath the tough exterior I discovered the usual cross-section of ordinary people: proud, vulnerable, insecure, humoursome, serious and funny, the casual, the fearful, the suggestible and every other variety of human being found anywhere. I found that paradoxically some of the toughest looking were the most gentle and when they talked and confided in me, as some did from time to time, I admired their honesty and gained an insight into their world. While not exactly mixing with the 'toughies', the smaller group of youngsters from the middle-class respectable church-going families of the parish that stayed in the club lived well with them. They shared adolescence in common: a contempt for the values, attitudes and beliefs of their parents and an unshakable belief in their own opinion on everything, coupled with a determination to explore the world on their own account.

They weren't all 'saints' however. On one occasion I visited a youth club member in Crumlin Road, the first time I had ever been in a prison. Little did I know that many years later I would be chaplain to Mountjoy Prison in Dublin. When I went to Crumlin Road to visit Danny, a warder with a big bunch of keys on his belt led me across a large courtyard to a door at the far end. When we went through the door he locked it behind us. This was the warder's normal workplace which was to me the strangest place I had ever been. All around there were tall stone walls and formidable metal doors. I was reminded of Wilde's 'little tent of blue we prisoners call the sky'. The warder led the way down a stone passage through another heavy metal door, which again he locked behind us, to a room with nothing but a table and two chairs.

'If you wait here.' The warder said and left me alone.

I sat down on one of the chairs and tried to imagine what it was like to be a prisoner. I knew the parts of the prison I had just seen were not normally frequented by prisoners, so the images I had of prison were from films; the bed, the small high window and the pot. I could feel the humiliation and shuddered. I knew that my upbringing meant that it was well nigh impossible for me to end up in prison, but I was also aware that the upbringing of some people meant it was virtually impossible for them not to end up in prison. It didn't seem fair that some people had every chance and some had no chance at all. As I mused on freewill and determinism I heard footsteps approaching, and the warder let Danny into the room and left, leaving the door open.

I didn't know Danny well, but he knew who I was. I stood up and put out my hand.

'How'ya Danny?'

Danny said nothing but nodded his head slightly. I sat down and Danny stayed standing. He wore shoes with raised heels and platform soles and at that he was no more than five feet two. He was strongly built and had thick black hair and a round face. He wore jeans, a tee shirt and a grey sweater.

'Why not sit down?' I said. He did.

'Some of your friends in the Club told me you were here. I hope you don't mind me coming to visit.'

Danny, who still hadn't spoken shook his head slightly.

'How long more will you be?' I asked, and immediately felt for some reason I shouldn't have.

'Two months and a bit.'

'Will you come back to the Youth Club then?' I asked.

Danny nodded his head and said 'OK.'

I was conscious of the image Danny must have had of me in dark suit and clerical collar. An image of clergy that militated against me gaining his confidence. I didn't know exactly what he was in for and I was careful not to say anything that would make me seem prurient. I had no way of knowing whether Danny's quietness was just Danny or whether the circumstances and the company induced it. I couldn't tell how he was coping with imprisonment and whether he had ever been there before, and while feeling sorry for the small bereft looking figure at the far side of the table, I had a sneaking suspicion that butter would have no trouble melting in his mouth.

Having run out of things to say I stood up.

'Would you like me to come and see you again?'

'If you like.'

'Is there anything I can do for you in the meantime?'

'Have you a fag?'

'I'm sorry, I don't smoke.'

I took out a half crown and gave it to him.

'Would that be any use?'

'Thanks.' He said, putting it in his pocket.

Danny left and the warder took him back.

Outside on the footpath, I stood and watched the normal world go by before going to my car.

In due course Danny did come back to the Club but no word passed between us about my visits to him in prison.

A choir in a parish makes a significant contribution to the quality of worship, and St John's had a good choir of ladies, gentlemen and boy sopranos – one of the best in the diocese. Good church organists are notoriously temperamental and the organist and choirmaster of St John's was good. He had high standards and he expected the same high standards of everybody else.

One evening I decided I ought to put in an appearance at choir practice in the choir vestry. I slipped into the back un-noticed and listened. Since the choir was standing the organist at the piano at the front did not see me. They were in full flight in an anthem so I sat back, closed my eyes and was absorbed in the music. Suddenly there was an almighty crash as the organist brought his fist down full force on top of the piano. I jumped a foot in the air. The singing stopped.

'Tenors, can you not count?' The organist roared. There was dead silence. 'One two and in on three.' He shouted, and moder-ating his volume but not his tone: 'If you want to sleep go home to bed. Now we'll take it from the bottom of the page again.'

Drowned in the rustling of the pages, a voice from the tenors whispered: 'You little bollocks.' And the singing started again. My heartbeat had just settled down when they came to the end of the anthem.

'Now the hymns,' the organist said as one of the choir collected the anthems. They rehearsed four hymns and then to a signal I didn't see, the practice broke up. Some of the choir spoke to me and asked if I sang. 'I do,' I said, 'But I'm not a singer.'

I approached the organist. 'I appreciate you coming,' he said. Which was a dig at the rector who was almost tone deaf and left the music entirely to the organist. And then he said, 'Do they not teach you anything about hymns in that college?'

'In fact they don't,' I said, 'I think that's something we're supposed to pick up as we go along. I think, however, it's important to have hymns the congregation knows and can sing,' a view that 'performing' choirs don't always support.

'But there are some fine new hymn tunes,' he said.

'But they're no use if the congregation can't sing them. Anyhow it's the theology of the hymns that bothers me more than the tunes.' A comment received in silence. The average church organist is not noted for his knowledge of theology. This conversation was a typical interaction between a good church organist and a musically illiterate cleric.

Church organists can be inflexibly purist. I was once at a country funeral when the congregation dragged one of the hymns so badly that the organist had finished the last verse when the congregation were just finishing the second last one. The organist played the last verse again and still finished before them.

One Sunday shortly after the rector came back from holiday, in the vestry after service the churchwarden, when he had finished counting the collection, said to the rector for me to hear:

'Well, rector, we'll have a new recruit here.'

I felt that I had been recruited five years ago and that I was already soldiering. The rector's response made it clear to me that it was to the Orange Order the churchwarden referred. The rector, knowing my views, made it clear that the new curate would not be 'taking the shilling'. The matter was never mentioned again. The rector himself joined the Orange Order when he went north as a young curate, not that he was an Orange type Protestant, but as a stranger in a strange land it was, as he said, a way of getting to know some of his male parishioners. There was no Orange Order Lodge connected with the parish as far as I knew. I assumed that parishioners were members of a Lodge somewhere in the district. In due course, when the troubles got into their stride in the early seventies, in common with many other clergy, I understand, the rector let his membership lapse and was no longer active.

I usually took my holidays in July and went south, so apart from this incident I only once encountered anything Orange. In my first August in the north, one day driving home from town I came upon a march. The traffic stopped and pulled in to the side. I had seen photographs in the paper but I had never seen the real thing before. Banners, a band, bowler hats, sashes, rolled umbrellas and faces fixed with expressions of serious intent. To me it seemed faintly ridiculous for grown men to behave in this way, but so serious were they that I realised it was a ritual of a culture of which I knew nothing. The rector subsequently explained that what I had seen was a Black march and not an Orange march. Black or Orange it was all very strange to me. I have never understood why people, of whatever political or religious colour, want to desport themselves in public in this way.

When I was at St John's about a year I was approached by the headmaster of the local Grammar School. He asked me if I would teach religious education one morning a week. Never having taught I was glad enough of the opportunity to see if teaching was for me, so I agreed. I taught five periods to 4th, 5th and 6th forms between 9.00am and 1.00pm with a quarter hour break, and then went home to bed. No matter how well I prepared I was exhausted. After a few weeks Hilary, who is a teacher, helped me with a few tricks of the trade. Don't give them so much concentrated material, break the class up with plenty of discussion and, when wilting, give them some written

work to do and sit and have a rest, and think of your next holiday or anything else that takes your fancy.

In the staffroom at break on the second morning the headmaster came in and gave me half a dozen forms to bring home to
sign. When I looked at the forms that evening there was
amongst them an oath of allegiance to the Queen. I took it out,
signed the rest and gave them to the headmaster at break the
next week. The following week he came into the staffroom again
and gave me another oath of allegiance saying:

'You missed this one. Perhaps you would sign it now.'

'I'm sorry headmaster,' I replied, 'I'm not prepared to sign it.'

'Oh,' he said, taken aback. 'Then I don't think the Education
Department will pay you.'

'Well that's all right,' I said. 'When you asked me to teach
you didn't mention money and I didn't expect to be paid.' And
off he went.

The next week at break he arrived into the staffroom again
and asked me if I would call to the Corporation Education
Department to speak to an official he named. I began to explain
my lack of concern about the money when he interrupted me
and said:

'Please do.'

Wishing to make as little fuss as possible I agreed. During the
week I called to the Corporation and asked for the official. I gave
my name. He leaned across the counter and said under his
breath:

'I understand you don't want to sign the oath.'

'That's right.'

'That's very unusual for a man in your position.'

'It's not a problem,' I said, 'as I'm not concerned about the
money.'

'Well thank you for coming in,' he said, and as far as I was
concerned that was the end of it.

In the meantime the headmaster had spoken to my rector,
though I didn't know what passed between them, and he arrived into the staffroom yet again the next week. By this time he

must have wondered what kind of subversive he had on his hands. He gave me the name of an official in the Ministry of Education at Stormont and asked me if I would call to see him. I told him I wanted to let the matter drop but he asked me in a very kindly way if I would do as he asked.

I called to the Ministry and asked for the official. He took me out of the office onto the landing, out of earshot, and told me he understood absolutely how I felt. We talked for a few minutes and he thanked me for coming. At least somebody, no doubt a nationalist, understood.

The headmaster did not arrive in the staffroom the following week, and very soon I received a cheque for arrears of pay and I was paid regularly after that.

I discovered later that teachers in England were not required to sign an oath of allegiance to the Queen, and in Northern Ireland the oath was abolished some years later.

CHAPTER EIGHT

St John's

So busy was I at St John's, and so full of enthusiasm for the work, that at first I didn't reflect on what I was doing. I just got on with the job I was presented with and enjoyed it. I enjoyed meeting people, working with people and supporting people through the traditional life of the parish. When I did think, I wondered what it was all about. I wondered when I saw two sworn enemies kneeling at the same communion rail. I wondered when I heard people talking about Roman Catholics as if they were lesser beings and outside the Christian imperative to love one's neighbour as oneself.

Talking to a Sunday School class of nine and ten year olds, I told them the story of the Good Samaritan and what it meant. I then asked them if they were going up the Newtownards Road and came across a Roman Catholic boy who had been knocked off his bike, was beaten up and robbed, would they help him? They all shouted 'No'. They didn't make the connection, which was probably my fault, or they gave me the answer they thought I expected. I was curious when I began to realise that for many people going to church was a ritual, and the content of what went on at the ritual didn't seem to impinge on them. Churchgoing seemed to be largely an affirmation of tribal loyalty. I wondered about some people's obsession with personal salvation – avoiding hell and getting to heaven. I wondered about these and many other things to do with the Christian faith. In fact I had many questions and few answers.

I had never found believing easy, especially believing in the miraculous aspects of the faith – the virgin birth, the resurrection and miracles. One of our professors in Divinity School,

Professor Vokes, in a lecture had raised the question gently about the historicity of the Virgin Birth and all hell broke loose. Evangelical students were scandalised, he was reported to bishops and questions were asked in synods as to his suitability to teach Church of Ireland ordinands.

Honest to God, by John Robinson, the Church of England Bishop of Woolwich, was published in my second year in college. In it he looked at modern developments in theology – God, Jesus and 'The New Morality'. In his preface he quotes a broadcast by Alec Vidler, a theologian, for which Vidler was bitterly attacked. He had said:

'We've got a very big leeway to make up, because there's been so much suppression of real, deep thought and intellectual alertness and integrity in the church.'

Robinson goes on to say:

'I am not in the least accusing of dishonesty those who find the traditional framework of metaphysics and morals entirely acceptable (I do with a large part of myself). What dismays me is the vehemence – and at bottom the insecurity – of those who feel that the faith can only be defended by branding as enemies within the camp those who do not.'

The book was 'a personal confession of convictions borne in upon him by the need to be utterly honest about the terms in which the faith can truly be presented today.'

This all rang true to me. I had no clear-cut answers for myself, but some beliefs expressed in traditional terms I found hard to accept and some new ways of understanding those beliefs made sense to me. I too was dismayed at the vehemence of people of traditional views in the face of honest attempts by others to make sense of Christian doctrines from a different perspective.

Most of the energies of the church were taken up with ensuring the survival of the institution and with observing rituals. The number of people who attended services and the success of the parish organisations measured the well-being of the church. Parishioners listened to sermons about what Christians believe and how they ought to work out their faith in their lives, and before they were home, or sometimes before they left the church, they had largely forgotten what was said. So too, probably, had the preacher of the sermon.

One conclusion I did come to was that, since the only way to change things for the better in society at large was through the political process, Christians should join political parties. Especially they should, as individuals, make their influence felt for the welfare of the poor and the underprivileged. The reported statement of Our Lord, 'The poor you will have always with you', does not absolve us from supporting the poor and trying to improve their condition. I had a tremendous sense of the inequalities in society and in the world at large. The same principle applied to many of the problems of the world: God did not seem to intervene; only the political process could change them. Praying in church for the starving millions and then going home to a fine Sunday lunch seemed almost a blasphemy, and a salving of conscience, but then sometimes one was helpless to do more. A Christian can of course give money, and many do generously, but Christians should also, as individuals, become involved in politics which is the only way that society's problems have any chance of being solved. Since I had no desire to be involved in politics in the north, and since I had decided that after a three-year curacy I would return to the south, I joined as a Head Office member of the Irish Labour Party. Not that I was naïve enough to believe that my joining the Irish Labour Party was going to solve much, but more of that later.

In the meantime, events in Northern Ireland were becoming, to say the least, heated. Unionists were attacking Civil Rights marches. Things came to a crisis with the Battle of the Bogside on the heels of an Apprentice Boys march on 12 August 1969. The victory of the residents over the RUC by excluding them from the area provoked a violent reaction amongst Protestants throughout Northern Ireland. Riots took place in many centres, especially in Belfast. On the night of 14 August some of the worst riots took place in the Falls-Shankill area and the following morning six people were dead and factories and over 100 houses had been destroyed, and many more had been damaged by petrol bombs.

In East Belfast over the following nights Protestant mobs tried to attack the small enclave of Catholics in Short Strand to burn them out. Throughout Northern Ireland the RUC and army were stretched beyond capacity and they were scarce on the ground. In the evening after work was the most dangerous time, and word went round amongst Protestant clergy in East Belfast to assemble on the Newtownards Road at the bottom of Templemore Avenue in the evenings at seven o'clock to try to help to calm the situation there.

One night at about ten o'clock, an angry Protestant mob assembled on the Newtownards Road ready to move down the road to attack the Catholics of the Short Strand. A line of clergy linked arms across the street to stop them. Initially the crowd was inhibited by this unlikely deployment of clerical collars, while we tried to reason with them. David Jardine, a native of Belfast, who was curate of the parish where we were, was beside me. He told me to keep my mouth shut, as if they heard my Southern accent they would attack me. He told me afterwards that he hoped nobody would use my name, as if they heard 'Paddy', they would think I was a priest from St Matthews, the local Catholic church. Then people at the back began to throw petrol bombs, most of which landed behind us. There was a sudden surge and the mob broke through. They ran up a side street but found their way blocked by an RUC roadblock.

Months later my name was useful to a couple who wanted to have their baby baptised 'Patrick'. When I told them that it was my name they were delighted to be able to tell their friends and family, who were mocking them for choosing a 'Fenian' name, that the clergyman who would baptise their son had a 'Fenian' name too!

Another night at the bottom of Templemore Avenue about midnight, a threatening crowd milled around. We clergy filtered through them trying to get them to disperse. Gordon McMullen, a Church of Ireland clergyman, later Bishop of Down, who came from the area and was well known to many of them, arrived and tried to get them to disperse, but they wouldn't. Things were looking ugly when out of the blue Paisley arrived on the scene with a few henchmen. He stood up on a pillar, spoke to the crowd, led them in the hymn 'O God our Help in Ages Past', and told them to go home. In two minutes the road was deserted.

One night in the small hours of the morning, walking home with a colleague after a night on the Newtownards Road, as we crossed Beersbridge Road there were 'B' Specials deployed at intervals along the street. They stood with their backs to the wall looking very nervous. I spoke to one of them. He had an ancient looking rifle and wore a uniform that was too big. He told me they were from a country area in mid-Ulster. A lorry had collected them that night; they were issued with a gun and a uniform and dropped on the Beersbridge Road. Before I said a word to this man, he had asked in a frightened way: 'Is this a Catholic or a Protestant area?' I had to think for a moment and told him it was Protestant. He shouted the information to his comrade-in-arms up the street. We talked for a while and then left the sleeping Beersbridge Road in the nervous hands of the 'B' Specials.

In due course a peace committee was formed on the Newtownards Road. Local clergy, on a rota, patrolled the area in the evenings with prominent local citizens in the hope of creating an atmosphere of calm and normality.

During this time, apart from 'Isn't it awful?' comments, I only remember one parishioner talking to me about the situation. She was genuinely puzzled as to why nationalists were marching and protesting. 'Wasn't everything all right before all these protests started?' she said, and believed it. I found it impossible to get her to see things from the nationalists' point of view. Her attitude was that they were lucky to be living in Northern Ireland with all the benefits of the welfare state available, and if they didn't like it couldn't they go to the south and live in poverty under the heel of the Catholic Church. I gave up.

When things settled down, as part of a public relations policy, the army made themselves available to work with young people.

Tommy, the leader of the parish Youth Centre, arranged for the army to take the Youth Club away to County Antrim on an adventure weekend and the rector decided that I should go too.

The youngsters piled into the bus outside the church early on Friday evening and in due course arrived at what looked like a converted coastguard station. It was a long two-storied stone building with a large room on either side of a stone archway. There was a long flagged kitchen with two big sinks, steel worktops and an institutional cooker in the middle of the floor.

It was dark and cold by the time we arrived, but there was a big open fire in one of the downstairs rooms. The leader gave a briefing and allocated the rooms: boys on one side of the arch and girls on the other. The village, about a mile away, and therefore the pub, was out of bounds, which meant an informal evening of television, table tennis or pool.

I sat beside the fire leaving everything to the leaders, who joined me when everyone had settled in. Feeling relaxed and without responsibilities, I went to bed. The room was cold and Spartan after the fire: a bed, a chair and a threadbare mat on the floor. I got into bed and fell asleep.

The next thing I knew was a loud knocking on the door.

'Who is it?'

'It's me, Tommy.'

I opened the door.

'They're running riot, can you help?'

I pulled trousers and sweater on over my pyjamas and set off with Tommy.

Still half asleep I could hear shouting and running and banging of doors. Along the corridor we met another of the leaders, neither he nor Tommy had been to bed and they discovered that the rapport they had established with the boys in the club did not seem to extend to a weekend away. Things were out of hand. Around the corner two boys came running at full tilt, one brandishing a chair leg. Tommy took the chair leg and ordered them back to their room. We set about checking each room for the right number of occupants. Some had none and one had four and a strong smell of beer but none in evidence. We were making some progress when I went into one room to find 'Stormy', the gang leader, who had appropriated to himself a single room, in bed with one of the girls, Jennifer. They were only partially covered. They pulled the bedclothes up and the girl turned her head away while 'Stormy' stared at me defiantly.

'Go back to your room immediately,' I said.

In a minute she came out dressed, sheepish and pale as a sheet.

After about half an hour there was calm. We patrolled the corridors until we were sure the storm had passed. Then we went downstairs and sat by the embers to put our thoughts together. We decided there was no point sending Stormy or Jennifer home. Stormy would probably refuse to go, and if we insisted most of the others would probably leave with him. We decided that on Monday evening Tommy and I would have to see Jennifer's parents. We didn't plan to go to Stormy's parents. Similar to the woman found in the act of adultery and brought to Jesus. Where was the man?

The most serious possibility was that Jennifer might become pregnant and, whether she did or not, these events might scupper the Youth Club in the parish. It would add fuel to the fire of those begrudgers who maintained that the parish Youth Club should be for the children of churchgoing parishioners only. As they would see it it was a case of 'what is the point of being respectable if your children have to mix with the hoodlums, vandals and fornicators of the area?' After all, isn't churchgoing about being respectable?

The following morning was fine, bright and sunny. It was perfect for the outdoor programme the leaders had arranged. The sea, seen from the dining-room at breakfast, was calm and glistening. The women leaders reported all quiet on their landing last night. They hadn't missed Jennifer nor did they see her arriving back.

Canoeing and abseiling were the two morning options. I chose to accompany the abseilers, determined I wasn't going to end up in water. A dozen of us headed off in the army truck with a sergeant and a corporal to a quarry a couple of miles away. I was tired from the night before and sat down and watched the others descend the rock face like flies.

'Come on, it's your turn.' A couple of slips of fourteen year old girls came running over to me and began to pull me up. Afraid of heights, I resisted.

'If we can do it, you can do it,' they taunted.

'I'm bad on heights,' I said, but they wouldn't take 'no' for an answer.

'It isn't high. Anyway you can't fall, there's a rope around you and you're held.'

The sergeant was manning the rope at the top.

'Come on,' he said. 'You'll be all right. Nothing can go wrong. It's safe as houses.'

'Come on,' the girls cried, and the eyes of the whole group were on the cowardly curate. I tried to comfort myself with the thought that if these young things, as they said themselves, could do it, why shouldn't I?

I went to the top of the rock face and looked over. It was a long way down. A shock of nerves pierced my stomach. The sergeant was already fixing me into the harness and telling me what to do.

'Turn and face me. Don't look down. Push yourself out from the face with your feet and take it in short stages.'

I knew with one part of me the soldier wouldn't let me fall, but with another part I was scared stiff. I turned and stood to the very edge and, still looking up, let myself down five or six feet. A cheer went up from the youngsters looking over the top. I felt pleased with myself but made the fatal mistake – I looked down. A surge of fear coursed through my body. I fought to control my bowels and just about succeeded. Then I froze. I could hear the sergeant shouting above me, but all I could do was look at my bloodless hand holding the rope in front of me.

'Look up, look up at me.' The sergeant shouted and I had the irrational fear that if I looked anywhere but at my hand I would end up in a heap at the bottom of the quarry. I eventually forced myself to look up.

'Can you come and get me?' I shouted.

The youngsters laughed.

'It is impossible for you to fall,' he said slowly. 'I won't let you. Now flex your knees, push out from the face and loosen your grip at the same time.'

I heard what he said but then my mind went blank except for the thought that as long as I kept a tight grip on the rope I wouldn't fall until someone came to rescue me.

Eventually the sergeant talked me through it again and made a tasteless joke about sending for a helicopter. I looked up and pushed myself out on a practice run. Then I did it again and loosened my grip. I landed safely a few feet further down. I looked straight ahead, repeated the operation and gained another few feet.

'You're nearly there,' a shout came from on top.

I made another jump and could see the ground four or five feet below me. One more jump and I would never do the likes of this in my life again. I pushed myself off, forgot to loosen my grip and landed back where I was. I did it correctly and landed on the ground beside the two girls who had come down to meet me. Another cheer went up on top and I sat down on the ground for no other reason than that my legs were so shaky I couldn't stand.

The girls helped me out of the harness.

'Now that wasn't so bad, was it?' one of them asked.

I eventually stood up on my watery legs and went back with the girls to the top of the quarry. I was sure that all eyes were on me, but already there were others having second turns.

'Well done, sir,' the sergeant said as I sat on the grass to recover.

The rest of the weekend went well but was ruined for me every time I though that Tommy and I would have to go and see Jennifer's parents after we got back.

I was back in the parish in time for the evening service on

Sunday night. I invited the rector over to the house afterwards saying I wanted to tell him about the weekend.

'Can it not wait until the staff meeting on Tuesday morning?'

'I'm afraid it can't.'

I told him the weekend had been a success except for finding Stormy and Jennifer in bed. His approach was that you can't monitor youngsters every minute of their time away, and this kind of thing was the responsibility of the home and not the Youth Club. I was relieved, at least the rector was on our side.

On Monday evening I met Tommy as arranged and we talked in the car before going to Jennifer's house. I told him what the rector had said and he was prepared to go even farther.

'The best form of defence is attack. We should threaten to expel Jennifer from the club for bringing it into disrepute.'

'Then we'd have to expel Stormy and we know what that would mean: three quarters of the club would go with him, and why aren't we going to see his parents anyway?'

'He's over eighteen and responsible for himself, but we'll have to warn him that it's up to Jennifer's parents to pursue it or not.'

Neither of us knew Jennifer's parents. Her mother answered the door. We introduced ourselves and she knew immediately something was wrong.

'Is your husband in? We'd like to talk to you both together.'

The four of us sat in the sitting room.

'I don't know if Jennifer told you but we found her in bed with one of the boys at the weekend.'

Jennifer's mother put both her hands to her mouth and gasped. Her father, after a short pause, said:

'I hope you fellows tell these kids about contraception and venereal disease.'

It was clear that Jennifer had not told her parents, and it was also clear that her parents were not at one in dealing with it.

'We had to inform you officially and we will deal with the matter in the club.'

Neither parent asked for more information so we left feeling great relief that it was unlikely the matter would scupper the club. The parents' attitude meant the begrudgers in the parish might not even hear of it and, if they did, we had the rector on our side.

We never did speak to Jennifer as she never came back to the club. We had Stormy in as planned. He listened to what we had to say with an attitude of dumb insolence, and when we finished he said:

'Is that all?'

'Do you understand the position?'

'Of course I understand.'

'Then that's all.' And Stormy stood up and left.

During my time the Youth Club didn't go away on any more army sponsored weekends.

My contact with the Troubles during this time was slight, compared to clergy in the north over the next thirty years, almost all of which time I spent in the south. For most of those thirty years clergy in the north were burying parishioners who died violent deaths and supporting their grief-stricken families. They were ministering to those who had been maimed and injured and they were supporting families that lived in fear. Many of these clergy, of all denominations, especially those in difficult areas, were heroic.

I never intended to stay more than three years in the north. As the end approached I decided to take time out to try to work on some of the questions I had about my own faith and the ministry of the church. This eventually took the form of a year at the Divinity School of the University of Chicago. One parishioner told us she was glad we weren't going back to the south because of the terrible time Protestants have there. She somehow got it into her head that we were going to Canada and solemnly informed us we would be all right in Canada because the Orange Order was there.

In August 1970 Hilary and I set sail for the United States.

CHAPTER NINE

Chicago

We stand on the bridge of a freighter in mid-Atlantic searching for whale spouts. It is a long way from the troubled streets of Belfast. The vast expanse of ocean impresses, and yet it is but a small part of our world, a minute part of the immensity of our galaxy and less than the speck of a speck in the infinity of the universe. Thinking about the creator of this universe sending his Son at a particular time and to a particular place, to treat with the likes of us, beggars belief.

The captain is known in the Line as Mad Maxwell. The first officer is seasick for the first day and a half at sea and attributes it to having a 'sky pilot' on board. All of the crew are friendly and we have free run of the ship.

There are three other passengers on board for the voyage from Liverpool to Montreal. A young man just down from Cambridge on his way to Canada to a job with Oxford University Press, and two young women on their way to Vancouver on holiday. We eat at the captain's table with the officers, who are particularly relaxed, especially with the two young women, on whose coat tails the other three of us are invited to officers' cabins for drinks before meals.

We read and play cards, watch for whales, shearwaters and petrels, and after a storm rescue an exhausted sparrow from the deck. I have a sense of being watched! We keep the bird in a cardboard box, feed it and release it at first sight of land.

From Montreal we travel to London, Ontario to visit a member of the diaspora of my father's family, an uncle, an Anglican priest in the Canadian Church, now retired. He was a man who ploughed his own furrow. He was awarded the Canadian

Mental Health prize in 1950 for establishing clergy/doctor groups. He spent the last fifteen years of his ministry as chaplain to a large mental hospital where, as he said himself, he felt very much at home. He loved people but was puzzled by the institutional church. From there we made our way to Chicago and the University Divinity School.

The University of Chicago is in Hyde Park, a mixed race island in the middle of the South Side black ghetto. The campus was self sufficient, including its own police force. The only safe way without a car from the campus to down town was by suburban rail. Shortly after we arrived, before term, having been to a film down town, at about 10.00pm we hailed a taxi and asked for Hyde Park. The driver shook his head and drove away. We hailed another. 'Sorry Bud,' and he drove off. After dark cab drivers would not drive through the ghetto to Hyde Park. While in Chicago Hilary was advised to carry a gun, or at least to carry a gas canister against personal attack. She carried neither.

Even within Hyde Park it was dangerous, and more than once we were woken during the night by gunfire. One evening friends looked out their window at the sound of people running, to see a man gunned down by police. Robberies were frequent and we were advised never to carry less than ten dollars, since an assailant who got less might beat us up. Belfast and Chicago were different kinds of violence. We felt much safer in Belfast. One thing they had in common, however, was that some Protestants in Belfast used exactly the same language to describe Catholics as some whites in Chicago used to describe blacks: 'You can't trust them, they won't work, they're dirty, they breed like rabbits.'

We had planned that both of us could survive in Chicago on my World Council of Churches allowance, though the World Council disclaimed any responsibility for Hilary. As soon as we arrived someone advised her that with a degree and shorthand and typing she was eminently employable. She did a test at the University Employment Office and within forty-eight hours she had a job as secretary to one of the professors of medicine at Billings, the University Hospital. She was paid almost three times my allowance, and that enabled us to turn the prospect of frugality into a time of plenty.

Chicago University is a prestigious graduate school and so my student friends at the Divinity School were bright young things in their early twenties from all over America. It was not a Divinity School geared to preparing people for ordination. It offered masters and doctorate degrees in anything from the text of the New Testament to religion and literature, from Buddhism to folk religion, the last of which, coming from Ireland, attracted my attention.

I was a 'Student at Large' for a year, which allowed me to pick and choose what courses I wanted to take. Amongst these were two courses on Reinhold Niebuhr's *Nature and Destiny of Man*, taught by Al Pitcher, who was an adviser to the Rev Jesse Jackson who first came to notice as leader of 'Operation Breadbasket', in the aftermath of a famous Martin Luther King rally in Chicago. I also looked at part-time ordained ministry, which was well established in a number of Protestant Churches around Chicago. This was at a time when part-time ministry was just being mentioned in the Church of Ireland. In due course the Church of Ireland trained and ordained men, and more recently women, to function as Auxiliary priests while holding down a full-time job. Auxiliaries make a significant contribution to the ordained ministry of the church. There is a New Testament precedent – St Paul, who made his living as a tentmaker while on his missionary journeys.

What I learned in formal courses was good, but so too was all that I learned informally from my young American student colleagues. About half them were young women, high on feminism. They were lively, intelligent and indulgent of this dinosaur from Ireland among them. Having been brought up by a feminist, before the word was fashionable, I had always considered myself a feminist, insofar as it is possible for a man to be one. I wasn't prepared, however, for the onslaught I encountered, from not only students but from female faculty members as well.

Having been brought up male in a conservative society, I was unconscious of many attitudes and actions of mine that feminist women found patronising and condescending, such as standing up when a woman entered or left the room, or holding open a door for a woman. These were not significant in themselves but reflected an attitude that was ingrained in me from childhood. These young women were in the first flush of asserting their newfound feminist freedom in a male dominated world and lost no opportunity to assert themselves and their cause. They did it mostly with humour but with unmistakeable seriousness. By the end of the year I had been re-educated to a moderate feminism, somewhere between my mother's unselfconscious version and that of my radical student friends.

The congregation of the local Anglican Church we attended in Hyde Park was a far cry from that of the average Church of Ireland church. There were all sorts and conditions of men and women from the four corners of America and around the world, professors, lecturers, students, administrators, cleaners. The church was modern and circular. The liturgy was High, always the Eucharist, celebrated in a way that would scandalise most Church of Ireland lay people: vestments, incense, genuflecting and the sign of the cross. The liturgy was alive: the ritual reflected the diversity of the congregation and the sermon was no more than five minutes.

At the Divinity School Hilary and I, as Irish Anglicans, were something of a curiosity. In America Irish means Catholic, and southern Irish certainly does. We in fact gravitated towards some Boston Irish American Catholic priests and nuns at the Divinity School, and they towards us. One of the priests, Jim Carroll, had been involved with Daniel Berrigan in his anti-Vietnam War campaign and has since left the priesthood and become a well-known author. They were alive and revelled in the freedom to grow and develop and study that Vatican II had given them.

Hilary and I wanted to get out of Chicago for the Christmas break. We phoned the Wisconsin Tourist Board to ask if they had farmhouse holidays like those in Ireland.

'Indeed we do, Sir.'

We chose a farm in the north of Wisconsin outside the small town of Medford. Two days before Christmas, we travelled north by Greyhound bus packed with people with parcels on their way home for Christmas, through countryside covered by a blanket of deep snow. As darkness fell, Christmas tree lights twinkled from windows of houses as we made our way through this fairyland to our unknown Christmas retreat. Helen Staab, the woman of the house, met us at the bus station with a warm motherly welcome and drove the six or seven miles to her typical American farmstead of clapboard house, barns, and a huge silo. So deep was the snow we could see only the tops of the fence posts around the garden. Jake, her husband, welcomed us every bit as warmly as Helen did and served us a hot supper.

Next morning we explored the farm in the intense cold. The cattle were in for the winter and all Jake's chores were around the farmyard. They had built their own barns; they shot their own venison, cured their own bacon and tapped their own maple trees for syrup. Jake showed us how to use a snowmobile which we drove up and down the frozen river that ran close to the house. In winter Helen could visit her mother by snowmobile on the river in half the time it took her by road at other times of year. No matter how well wrapped up we were in the snowsuits they lent us, we were glad to get back to the warmth of the house after even a short time outside.

On Christmas Eve adult children with spouses arrived. We felt like cuckoos in the nest, but everything the family said or did reassured us that we weren't. On Christmas morning we went to church in Medford with one of Helen and Jake's daughters-in-law. When we arrived back, Hilary and I went upstairs to our room to let the family on with their Christmas. Half an hour later we were lying on our bed reading when a knock came to the door. It was Helen to know where we were. We were brought down to the sitting-room and included in the family Christmas. They made us feel that it was their privilege to have us for Christmas. There were presents for us under the Christmas tree. Such genuine hospitality is humbling.

When our time came to leave Chicago in June, the nuns we had come to know invited us to stay with them at one of their houses in Boston. It was a large house in Jamaica Plains where six nuns lived. All wore lay dress and taught in a local school.

On the night we arrived they had a big dinner party to welcome us and invited some of the priests who had been friends in Chicago. The Mother Superior from the mother house in Boston, beautifully presented in a well-cut suit, came to welcome us and thank us for coming to stay. They made us feel special and were delighted with the opportunity to celebrate our friendship.

They joked about, but made no fuss of, the fact that I was the first man ever to stay in one of their houses. The sister with the biggest bed gave it up to Hilary and me, and slept on a mattress on the floor in the room of one of the others. At the end of a marvellous evening we made our way to bed and went to sleep. In the small hours of the morning I woke and needed to go to the lavatory. I turned on the light and went out on the landing. The house was colonial style with a labyrinth of passageways, landings and stairs, and I eventually found what I was looking for. When I started back for my bedroom I got lost. Behind one of the doors Hilary was asleep and behind the other doors were sleeping nuns. I didn't look forward to having to explain myself if I pushed open the wrong door. This woke me up fully and I remembered I had left on the bedroom light. On hands and knees I looked under doors and was greatly relieved to find the right room.

Next morning was Saturday. Some of the sisters arrived down to breakfast in dressing gowns, wearing curlers and two of them smoking cigarettes. We had known some of them for almost a year and others for less than twenty-four hours. They were all equally relaxed in our company. I recounted my peregrination during the night to their great amusement. These post-Vatican II nuns, for all their informality, were none the less strongly committed to their vocations as teachers. By this time the loss of the formalities of their earlier religious life was no longer an issue for them. They were, however, hungry to know more about us and about Anglicanism and about our religious experience.

On Sunday morning we all went to Mass at Boston University where one of the priests was chaplain. It was vacation time so there was only a handful of students, a few faculty members, the sisters and Hilary and me. It was very warm. The celebrant was dressed in jeans and an open necked shirt and we stood around informally on a grass area outside a lecture room with trams going by on the road nearby. The altar was a small table, the wine was from the supermarket and the bread was a bap. When the celebrant came to the consecration he put on a small stole. We communicated each other by pulling a piece from the bap and passing the cup from one to the other. It was 1970 and to the rest it seemed the most natural thing in the world. To us it was a new and exciting way to celebrate the Eucharist. Before the Mass started we asked the celebrant if it would be in order for us to receive communion. He didn't understand the question. He made no distinction; anyone who wanted to communicate was welcome. For us it was special to take part in this way with people with whom we had shared so much.

On Monday we set out with Sister Madeline, in the convent car, for a few days in New Hampshire and Vermont. They wanted us to see New England and their hospitality knew no bounds. When we came to leave Boston for New York to join the *Niewe Amsterdam* for the voyage to Cobh, the sisters gave us presents, tokens of the loving spirit of these generous people.

On the second day out from New York on this luxury liner, a contrast from the cargo vessel on which we had travelled the other direction, the ship's programme included an item: 'Meeting for all Clergy on Board'. I turned up to find two others: the ship's chaplain, a minister of the Dutch Reformed Church, whom I never saw again, and a Father Holland, an Irish Holy Ghost Father, from Clonakilty, Co Cork on his way home on furlough from Brazil. For the rest of the voyage, Father Holland spent much of his time with us. We arranged to share a table for meals and spent the evening entertainments together. In his late forties, he was as progressive as our priest friends in Boston, bearing in mind these were still the times of Archbishop John Charles McQuaid, Archbishop of Dublin, when priests were priests and dressed and behaved accordingly. We talked together about many things and Fr Holland attributed his progressive ways to his years on the missions and to the younger post-Vatican II priests arriving in Brazil from Europe. He put it simply, saying that if he didn't move with the times he was in danger of being sidelined.

We arrived home in June 1971 having learned something of the churches in America and my having read some theology. Neither of these allayed the restless nature of my belief. After a year in Chicago I was no further on with some of my questions. I hadn't directly addressed issues like miracles, the virgin birth or the resurrection. I hadn't looked at the scandal of particularity – why God chose a particular time and a particular place to reveal himself in the person Jesus Christ – nor the theodicy problem – the difficulty of reconciling evil in the world with the existence of an all-loving all-powerful God. However, my attitude to all of these was evolving in the context of new experiences. Above all, I had developed the confidence to confront these issues for myself.

My time in America had been a breath of fresh air. I had met bright young people who were interested in theology for its own sake, rather than simply as a discipline to be studied for ordination. I had been introduced to refreshingly open approaches to liturgy. The churches in America were not weighed down by history or tribalism in the way the churches in Ireland were. Being Anglican I met Episcopalians and being Irish I met Roman Catholics. There was a great openness about the church people I did meet and they were open and trying hard to struggle with what it meant to be the people of God in a changing world.

As we sailed towards the Irish coast the first sight of land caused a ripple of excitement among passengers lining the rail on deck. A distant outline became larger, then slowly turned green. A green we hadn't seen since we left Ireland. For Hilary and me, away for only a year, it was exciting. What it must it have been like for some on board who had been in America for years, returning for the first time, I could hardly imagine. This gave us some slight insight into the pain of emigration and I knew then I could never live permanently outside Ireland. Unlike so many, I was fortunate that I didn't have to. I was glad to be home. For the moment I was unemployed until I could discover which vacant Church of Ireland parishes I might consider and which might be prepared to consider me.

CHAPTER TEN

The Church of Ireland

The Church of Ireland, as a member of the Anglican Communion, is one of a communion of national churches worldwide whose doctrine is that of the early church and whose reformed status derives from the English Reformation. All Anglican Churches are in communion with the Archbishop of Canterbury and with each other. During the English Reformation the reformers held that the doctrine, worship and day-to-day life of the church had become corrupt in a number of ways and were in need of reform to bring the church in line again with the teaching of the early church. The principle employed was that: 'Holy Scripture containeth all things necessary to salvation: so that whatsoever is not read therein, nor may be proved thereby, is not to be required of any man, that it should be believed as an article of Faith, or be thought requisite necessary to salvation.' That is not to say that everything in scripture must be believed, nor that things not provable by scripture may not be believed, but they are not necessary for salvation.

The Anglican Church is the Catholic and Apostolic Church reformed of errors that many believed had crept in in the Middle Ages. It was not a new church from the time of the Reformation, as some people claim. All doctrines of the early church are doctrines of the Anglican Communion and all doctrines of Anglicanism are doctrines of the early church.

In 1870 the Church of Ireland was disestablished and separated from the Church of England. It is administered according to a Constitution, amended from time to time by the General Synod. The guardian of the faith of the Church of Ireland is the House of Bishops, of whom the Archbishop of Armagh is a kind of first among equals. The final authority in matters of Order is the General Synod, which is composed roughly of two-thirds laypeople and one-third clergy and the House of Bishops.

Lay people have a central role in the administration of the church, especially in the local parish. The finance of a Church of Ireland parish is under the control of the Select Vestry, a committee of sixteen or more lay members, elected annually at a parish annual general meeting. The rector is chairperson but has no more say in deciding expenditure within the parish than any other member of the vestry, which makes decisions on a simple majority vote. The normal dynamics of any vestry operate sometimes in favour of the plans of a rector and sometimes against. How well a rector can politic and chair a meeting can sometimes determine what he can do. If a rector gets on the wrong side of the vestry, life can be difficult for him.

There are about 375,000 members of the Church of Ireland, of whom less than 100,000 live in the Republic, where it is the largest church of the minority of less than five per cent of members of all religions who are not Roman Catholic. In the Republic members are more sparsely distributed in the west and relatively more plentiful in the east. They are represented across the social spectrum from the descendants of the former ascendancy to urban poor, and are well represented in the farming community.

Church of Ireland members in the Republic are, by and large, not anti-Roman Catholic. However, in the face of an overwhelming majority of 95% Roman Catholics, and given the propensity of minorities to diminish, they have a strong motivation to survive as a community with a distinctive tradition, which in some of its manifestations may be interpreted as anti-Catholic. Relations between the two churches since Vatican II have been good. In recent times there has been an immense amount of support for each other between individuals and parishes of both traditions. I arrived back in Ireland in 1971 when this working together was beginning to happen, and within a few weeks I was appointed to the parish of Stradbally in County Laois.

Stradbally is a village seven miles from Portlaoise and seven miles from Athy in the centre of a prosperous farming community. The subsistence of the village in earlier days depended on three large estates. The antecedents of many of the residents, especially Church of Ireland families, worked on one or other of these estates. When we arrived in Stradbally one of them had been divided by the Land Commission and the house was a ruin, another very large house was surviving on a small amount of land and the third was working as a large modern farm. In the village there was a maltings, a stone works and a ladder factory that gave some employment, while a number of people went to Portlaoise or Athy for work.

Stradbally is famous for its Steam Rally, started by the colourful Captain Kidd who left his body to medical science. The clergyman taking his funeral service announced that mourners should not follow the hearse beyond Athy. This led to rumours that he wasn't dead at all and there were reported sightings of him for years afterwards.

There were four churches in the parish of Stradbally Union: St Patrick's in the village, Ballintubbert, Timogue and Luggacurren. Half of the parish had formerly been the Parish of Timahoe, of which a brother of my father had been rector in the 1930s. When war broke out he joined the British Army as a chaplain and exchanged the rural tranquility of Timahoe for the North Africa campaign, Italy and a prisoner-of-war camp in Germany.

The rectory was a medium sized late eighteenth century house of no distinction. It had, however, a fine drawing room that had been made of the former drawing room and dining room together. The ceiling had been raised to give the room its fine proportions. The whole floor area of the curate's house in Belfast was less than the size of this drawing room in Stradbally, which gives some idea of the problem of furnishing the rectory, despite a modest grant from the Church Body.

When we were leaving the north, we intended to go back to the south on our return from Chicago. We planned to store our furniture in Dublin, since the Troubles were under way in Belfast.

There was a last minute hitch with customs papers so we stored the furniture in Belfast and left for Dublin en route for Chicago. The following day the store our furniture would have been in in Dublin was burned to the ground. Pure chance. Half joke whole earnest, friends said things like, 'God looks after his own', and 'You must have been saying your prayers'. It would be whole joke no earnest to believe in a God that interferes in customs clearance procedures in order to save someone's furniture from destruction!

The furniture van had just left, having delivered our furniture from Belfast to the rectory, when there was a ring at the door. It was a man from the village to welcome us to Stradbally. I invited him in to the chaos. He sat down and launched into a long convoluted story the sum total of which was to ask if I could lend him ten pounds, which naturally he would pay back. I asked him tentatively if he was a Church of Ireland parishioner, knowing full well he wasn't. There was a convention amongst clergy about such matters, I told him. I would certainly help him, but first I would have to pay the parish priest the courtesy of telling him, as similarly he would tell me if a Church of Ireland parishioner approached him. He nearly knocked the phone out of my hand to prevent me dialling Father Mahon.

'No, no. It's all right,' and he was out the door like a shot out of a gun. I learned later that the said gentleman's nickname in the village was 'The Chance'!

The bishop was Henry McAdoo who arranged the service of my institution to the parish. He didn't consult me about the date! I was informed that it would be on a Sunday, which meant that none of my clerical friends or colleagues could attend. McAdoo was an Anglican scholar of international repute. He was joint chairman of ARCIC – Anglican Roman Catholic International Commission. He was an outstanding bishop but he never lost an opportunity to say how busy he was and what a full diary he had, to the extent that when asked for an appointment he offered dates in the distant future or else the opportunity to discuss immediately on the phone the most important of matters.

For a man of his ability he had a curious need to mention his scholarly achievements. When he retired, a number of bishops he had brought onto the bench took him out for a meal – an acknowledgment of his influence.

In the days that followed there were a number of callers to the rectory, some bringing their own produce, eggs and tomatoes and a welcome to the parish; we were well and truly in the country.

Shortly after we arrived I answered the door to a lady and gentleman in their seventies who were on holiday in the area. They were Mary Anderson and Alan Stewart, the daughter and son of a former rector, both of whom had been born in the house. We welcomed them and had coffee among the packing cases in the study. They told us stories of their childhood and the house as it had been in the first decade of the century and how their mother had died upstairs in the main bedroom at Mary's birth. She recounted a childhood hope for the second coming when she would look out the window and see her mother wafting up to heaven from the churchyard down the road and she would be gathered up to join her.

It transpired that Mary's late husband was a first cousin of my father, a cousin I didn't know I had. Almost every year while we were in Stradbally she returned for a holiday to a friend nearby, came to lunch at the rectory and tended the grave of her parents. She had overcome much adversity in her life. She regained sight in one eye having been totally blind for some time. The great thrills for her when this happened were seeing the faces of people she had met while blind and being able to drive again! Many years later, she ended her days with her son in County Cork and I was invited to return to Stradbally to speak and inter her ashes with her parents in the churchyard, and not a sign of the second coming.

Within a couple of weeks of our arrival Hilary and I received an invitation to a meal from the sisters of the Presentation Convent in the village. My predecessor, Walton Empey, had established a good relationship with them. We were delighted to be asked. When we arrived a sister brought us into the parlour where a number of the community were waiting to welcome us. We were given a drink – Hilary a glass of sherry, suitable for a clergyman's wife, and for me half a tumbler of Power's Gold Label. In the middle of the room a table was set for two on which a virtual banquet was laid out. We sat surrounded by the sisters, who had already eaten, and with every mouthful we took we were offered more. As I worked my way slowly through the whiskey I had a job to stop them replenishing it.

The warmth of the welcome and the hospitality were unstinting. They told us of their new ways since Vatican II. One of the older sisters, retired from teaching, described how after they were free to go out, and before the convent had a phone, she was called to take a phonecall at a shop across the road. She went to cross the street and had to go back into the convent to ask another sister to go with her, so frightened was she to cross on her own. The older sisters, some of whom had been in the convent for fifty and more years, were slow to adjust but the younger ones were glad of their newfound freedom.

We in turn told them of our life and experiences, especially of our time in America and our stay with the sisters in Boston. In deference to the older sisters we did not recount the curlers and the cigarettes at breakfast or my nighttime peregrinations in search of my bed.

Apart from fair days when I was a child in Wexford, I knew nothing about farming or farmers. I had lived all my life in town or city and I didn't know the difference between hay and straw. I would have known that a bullock was not a danger and a bull was, but I would not have been sure why. I soon realised that if I were to be any use to 95% of my parishioners I would need to know something about farming and understand their way of life. One Sunday I announced in church that because of my ignorance of farming I would like to do a day's work with any farmer parishioner that would have me. I wanted the farmer to show me his system but I wanted to help with the work of the day as well; to arrive in the yard at whatever time work started and to work that day's work whatever it happened to be on the principle: 'I hear, I forget; I see, I remember; I do, I understand.' There were no volunteers. They wondered what kind of fool had arrived as their new rector.

I approached one farmer I had come to know who readily agreed to my plan. I had a fascinating day. Word got around that I was serious and every couple of weeks over a period of months I did a day's farm work with a different farmer. I turned up in the yard early, suitably dressed, and Hilary came out in the evening to collect me. On more than one occasion I fell asleep at the evening meal I was so unused to hard physical work. I milked cows, bedded cattle, fed calves, fenced, drove tractors and on one occasion a combine harvester, and I gleaned information about grants from the EEC.

I learned that farmers work hard and long hours. I learned how dependent they are on the weather and how, apart from those in milk, some farmers get paid only twice a year, when they sell the cattle and after the harvest. I also learned two other interesting things. Work for a farmer means physical work; what people in collars and ties and clerical collars do isn't really work at all. The second is that no matter how well a farmer does he will never admit to making money. During this time I read *The Farmers' Journal* to keep abreast of what was going on in the world of farming.

After a curacy and a year for reflection I was now on my own to get on with the work where the essential task of the church takes place – in the local parish. Here I was in Stradbally in the midlands of Ireland to get on with the job. That job is simply the worship of Almighty God, to give God his worth or place in our lives. Not just formal worship as in the liturgy, but the giving of God 'worthship' in every aspect of life. The role of the clergy is to be the leader in liturgical worship, and to provide pastoral care. Administration is the necessary evil to make both of these possible.

The proportion of clergy time and energy spent on these three, worship, pastoral care and administration is in inverse proportion to their importance. To some people the parish means the buildings, the finance, the fund raising, the committees and all the other administration that is necessary, and they put on the good suit and go to church as well. Whereas the purpose of the church is worship, and administration is a necessary evil. The Church of Ireland is structured in such a way that lay people do much of the administration but some clergy like to keep most of it to themselves as a means of control. Give lay people too much control, some clergy would argue, and goodness only knows where you'll end up.

Then there are the lay expectations of what clergy should do and how they should behave. These expectations are not only of the clergy but extend to their families as well. Many's the rectory child has been scolded in school with: 'You did such and such and your father a clergyman.' The members of the rector's family are somehow supposed to be able to divest themselves of their humanity and be the infallible models of family life. Clergy are expected to be the role models for all behaviour and when they fail they are the worst in the world.

In a Church of Ireland parish the one thing clergy cannot fail to do is conduct the liturgical services of the church. After that they can do more or less whatever they like whenever they like. They can only be removed from office for dereliction of duty – if they neglect to take Sunday services, baptisms, weddings or funerals. They can also be removed for something like adultery or gross indecency. After the essentials it is up to each individual member of the clergy to decide how he or she spends their time.

If a doctor is negligent a patient may die, if an architect makes a mistake a building may collapse, or if an engineer is careless a bridge may fall down, but if a member of the clergy is negligent, makes a mistake or is careless nothing much happens. I know one clergyman who forgot a funeral but fortunately he was at home when someone came to find him. Many clergy, however, do work twelve or more hours a day, six days a week, especially in these days of shortage of clergy when they are often helping in vacant parishes as well as their own. There are some clergy who work so hard that they neglect their responsibilities as spouse and parent at a terrible cost.

As far as clergy are concerned there are different kinds of parishioner. There is one kind who, if the rector takes an afternoon off and is seen on a golf course or beside a river, will say their rector spends his time playing golf or fishing. Another kind of parishioner knows how hard clergy work and would encourage them to take more time off. Some parishioners have the 'holy' image of the clergy: good as gold, having no difficulty believing everything, pure in thought, in word and in deed and utterly harmless. Others understand that clergy are as human as anybody else.

Clergy, as individuals, are as different from each other as chalk is from cheese, both in personality and in their beliefs. The diversity that exists in the world at large exists among the clergy too, believe it or not. To hear some people talk you would think all clergy were the same. By subscribing to the same body of doctrine, they do not believe the same things in exactly the same way. The traditional categories of Anglican clergy are mentioned by John Betjeman in his poem 'House of Rest', talking of the widow of a vicar:

I do not like to ask if he
Was 'high' or 'low' or 'broad'
Lest such a question seem to be
A mockery of Our Lord.

Those with a high church bent stress the church's historical continuity with Catholic Christianity, and hence uphold a 'high' concept of the authority of the church. They emphasise the nature of priesthood, the episcopate and the centrality of the sacraments. Outward manifestations of this are ritual in worship and, in the past, they wore a black suit and a narrow collar. These days they wear dark colours and usually a tonsure collar.

Low church clergy give a 'low' place to priesthood, episcopate and sacraments and generally approximate in their beliefs to Protestant non-conformism. They are usually 'evangelical' in that they stress personal conversion and are strong on the inspiration and authority of the Bible. In the past they used to wear grey suits and deep collars. These days they wear all kinds of everything. Some of them don't even wear jackets!

The rest are broad church. These object to a narrow definition in theology and seek to interpret church doctrine in a 'broad' sense. In other words, all those who aren't 'high' or 'low'. These usually dress moderately respectably.

In the Church of Ireland there is only a small number of high-church clergy and parishes. The outwardly low church character of the Church of Ireland is a reaction to the majority Roman Catholic position. It is interesting to note that in Scotland, where the majority church is Presbyterian, and therefore non-conformist, the Anglican Church is high.

Two other kinds of Anglicans are fundamentalists and liberals.

'Fundamentalism' is a twentieth century development within conservative evangelicalism to defend Protestantism against biblical criticism, theological liberalism and the theory of evolution.

Modern 'liberals' interpret doctrines as a result of the consequences of biblical criticism. In the Church of Ireland they are indistinguishable from 'radicals' who nobody knows what they believe, sometimes not even themselves.

A wise old archdeacon of the Church of Ireland, when discussing such matters, was wont to say that religion was 'a reverent exploration of the mystery that surrounds us.'

The poor unfortunate clergy cannot win, and the mistake many of us make is to believe that if we try hard enough and are cute enough we can. Clergy are recruited from the ranks of the laity and, believe it or not, retain through ordination their humanity and all that that means. They are as human and diverse as any other group, but that doesn't suit some parishioners who project an unreal expectation on them to behave in a way they are unable to themselves. They want them to be vicarious perfection for them, and when they fail the same parishioners comfort themselves by criticising them. There are all kinds of lay people in parishes, which is not surprising when you reflect upon it and there are all kinds of clergy. It was summed up well by a wise young curate who, when his mother asked if the parishioners in his parish liked him, said: 'Some of them love me, some of them can't stand me and some of them don't give a damn one way or the other.'

Some lay people seem to believe that somehow it is the job of clergy to take any criticism they care to dish out. They believe that as a priest, if you put yourself up there, you are fair game. You are not supposed to have feelings or to hurt like other human beings. None the less I have no doubt that clergy can cope better with what lay people say about them than lay people could cope if they knew what clergy sometimes say to each other about them. The kinds of things a couple of clergy talking about lay people may say I will leave to your imagination.

Different clergy have different aptitudes and gifts they bring to their work. Like ordinary people, they fill, as best they can, their own personality needs through their work. No more than anyone else, they haven't got pure motives unadulterated by their own human needs and instincts.

Where do bishops fit in? Just as clergy are recruited from the ranks of the laity, so bishops are recruited from the ranks of the clergy. Bishops of the Anglican Communion are in continuity with the historic episcopate of the undivided church. The episcopate is one of the badges of the Catholicity of Anglicanism. The fact that the Roman Catholic Church does not officially acknowledge that this is so creates problems for ecumenism between the two churches. It is surprising how such unprovable abstruse theological issues become so important to intelligent grown men on both sides. All such matters become very theological and it is interesting to note that the word 'theological' in ordinary English today has come to mean 'abstract gobbledygook'.

A body made up of bishops, clergy and laity appoints bishops in the Church of Ireland. Before their meeting they celebrate the Eucharist and pray for the guidance of the Holy Spirit on their deliberations but this does not preclude canvassing, politicking and manoeuvring before and during the process. Some clergy from early on in their careers set their minds on becoming bishops and every move they make is designed towards that end. They pursue their careers in such a way as to promote their chances of episcopal appointment or, to put it at its least, they will do nothing to harm those chances. One curate whose rector did little to conceal his episcopal ambition, used to warn people on their way to the rectory not to trip over the bags in the hall. This particular man eventually did pack his bags and turned out to be a good bishop, and he clearly enjoyed every minute of it.

I suppose it is arguable that in order to be a good bishop one needs that kind of motivation. By and large in my time good people have been appointed bishops. Some clergy who haven't planned and hoped for appointment have been elected bishops to their own surprise and the surprise of everybody else, so maybe the Holy Spirit does get his way in the end. However, since being 'safe' is almost invariably a *sine qua non* for being elected a bishop, I have no doubt that if Jesus were around in the flesh today he would have no chance of becoming a bishop in the Church of Ireland!

The same kind of politicking and manoeuvring that takes place in episcopal appointments also takes place for appointments to lesser preferments – deaneries, archdeaconries and canonries. Bishops, however, make most of these appointments, which may be the basis for the belief that after a man becomes a bishop he will never hear the truth again. Some deaneries and canonries are historical hangovers and are no more than rewards for long service. In fact, in some western dioceses of the Church of Ireland there are almost as many canonries as there are clergy.

It is against this background that a rector starts his work in a new parish. Only the years have borne these realities in on me. I was oblivious to them when I started in Stradbally in 1971. An innocent abroad, I had it all to learn. But despite all of these things the game is well worth the candle. There is nothing to compare with the privilege of being with people and families through the rites of passage – baptism, marriage, death – and supporting people through problems and crises in their lives. It is a tremendous privilege to be with people through difficulty and tragedy and to be able to celebrate with them in their joys.

CHAPTER ELEVEN

Stradbally

In the nineteenth century it may have been close to the truth to say that clergy worked only one day a week. Today clergy like to believe that people say this only in jest, though one suspects people sometimes mean it. The truth is that, like a woman's work, clergy's work is never done. Furthermore these days there are fewer clergy doing more work. How then do they spend their time?

The first task of clergy is to conduct, and preach at, the liturgical services of the church. In city parishes, if there is a curate, this may mean the rector and curate each will have to preach only once on a Sunday. In many country parishes with a number of churches, the rector may conduct and preach at as many as four services on a Sunday morning, often driving up to fifteen miles between some of the churches. In some cases there will be another service in the afternoon. This kind of schedule is punishing for even the youngest and the toughest. In fact it is arguable that it is impossible for anyone to take more than three services in the day and conduct them properly, even if they use the same sermon, as they usually do. Why all these churches in the Church of Ireland? We have inherited them from another age when transport was the pony and trap, and they have become shrines for local communities.

In most of us there is but a thin veneer of Christianity on top of deep layers of tribal and primitive folk-religion. No matter how sophisticated we think our Christian faith is, we all respond some of the time with deep-seated folk-religion responses. Three components are essential to the well-being of the tribe: if the tribal priest performs the tribal ritual at the tribal shrine the well-being of the tribe is ensured. The tribal priests of the Church of Ireland are the episcopally ordained clergy. If a lay reader takes a service at holiday time or during a vacancy in a parish the people appreciate their help and they are grateful to have them for they have some service rather than none, but 'it's not the same'. It is second best to having a member of the clergy – a proper priest. The church itself which reserves certain functions, especially presiding at the Eucharist, to validly ordained clergy confirms this matter of the authentic priest.

The tribal ritual, until recently for most people and still so for some, was the service from the 1662 *Book of Common Prayer*. When the revised liturgies in modern English were introduced, many people were deeply upset and in some cases left parishes to go where they could find a *BCP* service. The new liturgies are faithful to the doctrines of the Church of Ireland. They are in modern English, easily understood, but some people still cannot accept them because they are not the service on which they were brought up. Some miss the beauty of the Tudor English despite archaic usage. There is a similar reaction by Roman Catholics who miss the Latin Mass.

Perhaps the angriest reaction of all comes when it is proposed that a church be closed. All kinds of rationalisations are bandied about against the case for closure: money, distance to travel to the nearest church, and many others. They all miss the point. What is happening is that the well-being of the tribe is being threatened at a deep primeval level by closing a tribal shrine. This affects people whether they attend church or not. In fact people who don't attend are often most upset and quote the rites of passage rituals. 'You can't close that church. All my family were baptised, married and buried there.'

One former Church of Ireland bishop, in a southern rural diocese, recounts that when a church came to be closed because of small numbers and the amalgamation of parishes, not only did the Church of Ireland parishioners become angry and protest to him vigorously, but he received a delegation of Roman Catholic parishioners, unbeknown to their Church of

Ireland neighbours, to appeal to him to keep the church open. The closure of a church has a profound affect on everybody, but unfortunately sometimes it has to be done.

If you have any doubt about the validity of the folk-religion principle you need look no further than Northern Ireland. There are two tribes both claiming allegiance to the same God, the summary of whose teaching is 'Love God and love your neighbour as yourself', and some of them hate each other's guts. Each tribe is threatened by the other and affirms its tribal allegiance, through its own rituals led by its own priests at its own shrines.

Many responses in the Christian community have their origin in folk-religion. This is not necessarily a bad thing in itself, unless perhaps where these responses are contrary to the apostolic faith. To understand the nature of folk-religion sometimes helps us to make sense of what is going on. One fine good Christian man I knew, when there was talk of the church he attended being closed, told the rector angrily, 'I don't care what you do inside that church. Just keep that bloody door open.' Do what you like inside my shrine but you'll threaten the life out of me if you close it. The shrine is where the rites of passage – birth, marriage and death – are performed even for those who don't normally attend. The fact that ancestors worshipped there for generations, are buried there and are commemorated on plaques on the walls, adds to its mystical importance.

After conducting worship, the next most important duty of the clergy is pastoral care. This includes everything that fosters membership of the parish from pastoral visiting to the activities of religious societies, to table tennis and bowls clubs. The first priority is the visiting of the sick, followed by routine visiting. Time was when Church of Ireland clergy gave high priority to visiting all of their parishioners routinely once a year. These days this is rare, and so busy are they that some clergy have stopped routine visiting altogether.

Meeting parishioners in their own homes gives clergy a chance to get to know them and they are more likely to come to church. The saying tells us: 'A house-going parson makes for a church-going people.' Visiting also means that if people know the clergy they are more likely to turn to them in a crisis. However, clergy are jacks of all trades and masters of none. For example, it was traditional in the past for the local rector to give a pep talk to a young couple getting ready for marriage. These days there are experts for this job and there is no reason in the world why clergy should claim to have specialist knowledge in this and in other areas. A parishioner whose marriage was in serious trouble once told me there would be no problem at all if his wife would only do what he told her. He was deadly serious. Expert or not, where would you begin?

A disproportionate amount of clergy time is spent on administering the parish and on the maintenance of churches, halls and rectories and since many of these are old buildings maintenance is a continuous job. Dublin Diocese in the last number of years experienced the opposite end of the spectrum. A virus was abroad in the diocese causing the building of new parish centres. A parish without a new parish centre was only in the ha'penny place. Buildings old and new, despite lay involvement, mean work for clergy that isn't mentioned in the ordination service.

Above all else, a primary school in the parish takes time. A school is the future of the parish but it means work and often it means trouble for clergy, especially when he or she is chairperson of the board of management. If teachers aren't the problem it's parents, if it isn't parents it's children. There's always some problem to deal with apart from routine administration.

It is time that the church withdrew clergy altogether from school management and if the church still wants control, and they do, they should leave it to lay people. The churches believe that control of schools is essential to promote their own distinctive ethos but this ought not to be at the expense of the well-being of the clergy. When it comes to schools the churches behave as control freaks. It's time for integrated education in Ireland. Let the churches themselves take responsibility for the religious education of their children outside school hours. Despite what some people, say there is no such thing as Roman Catholic or Church of Ireland maths or geography. It is not the subjects that are the problem but this mysterious 'ethos'. At present the Church of Ireland in the south is afraid of being swamped in a non-denominational educational world whereas it believes it can maintain its own ethos in its own schools. It is interesting to note that in the south many Roman Catholic parents choose to send their children to Church of Ireland managed schools, and I believe that this is good for the children of both traditions. In some cases Church of Ireland schools have to limit the number of non-Church of Ireland children they will take. This is an interesting phenomenon and perhaps someone ought to do some research to see what is really going on.

In a parish the rector is *ex officio* chairperson of the select vestry, elected once a year by the general vestry of all registered parishioners. The vestry is responsible for the three F's, finance, furnishing and fabric: all parish finance, the furnishing of churches and the fabric of buildings. The one area where the vestry does not have control is in the ordering of worship. If they did, the lives of many clergy would be intolerable.

By and large, vestries are supportive of their clergy but they don't relish having to raise money and so they are reluctant to spend it. One vestry had spent money doing some renovations to make the rectory habitable. When the rector's wife asked one of the glebe wardens responsible to the vestry for the rectory, if she could have a new lavatory seat as the old wooden one was cracked, his reply was, 'Aren't we doing enough for you?' Some vestries spend as little as they can get away with on rectories while others see it as their job to ensure that rectory families are comfortable in their houses and have, within reason, everything they need. A rectory family can be lucky or unlucky in who they have to deal with concerning the comfort of their home.

There is a high proportion of control freaks among treasurers of select vestries, some of whom see it as their job to tell the vestry how much money they can spend. Some people operate on the principle that you don't spend money you haven't got.

Others like to spend borrowed money on the principle that it is good for the *esprit de corps* of the parish to have a campaign of fund raising to pay off the dept. It is for the vestry as a whole to decide what money they spend and how to provide it, and for the treasurer to carry out their instructions.

Given the age of many Church of Ireland churches ... and here may I digress? To say 'Church of Ireland church' is correct. Almost inevitably newspapers, even *The Irish Times*, believe it or not, and radio and television, say that a funeral or wedding or other service took place in the 'Church of Ireland' such and such a place. The Church of Ireland is a national church and the building is a Church of Ireland *church*. The media should report events as taking place in the 'Church of Ireland church' such and such a place. Editors might like to take note.

Given the age of many Church of Ireland churches, vast sums of money are needed to keep them in repair. Serious money means a major fund raising drive. Small Church of Ireland communities are heroic in the generosity with which they contribute towards keeping their church open and in good repair. It sometimes happens that the local Catholic parish, in addition to supporting Church of Ireland fund raising, mounts their own fund raising event and the parish priest presents the rector with a substantial cheque to keep the roof on his church.

If it were not for the support in the south of Roman Catholics for Church of Ireland fêtes, bazaars and sales of one kind or another to raise money for current parish expenses, many small Church of Ireland country parishes would not survive.

One of the main fund raising events in Stradbally was the annual fête. It was held on Corpus Christi, a farm holiday. The shops in the village were open and the local curate at Mass that morning would encourage his parishioners to support the Church of Ireland fête. So strong a supporter was he that he would tell those who had to work to go up for a while to the fête and come back down and let others up to spend their money. This was in contrast to a parish priest in the same village some years before who forbade his parishioners to support the

Church of Ireland fête. One of his parishioners recounted to me, 'Most of us took no notice.'

Church of Ireland parishioners in Stradbally worked hard for their parish and particularly for the fête, while Catholic friends and neighbours manned some of the stalls. All of this made for excellent community relations, so much so that when the rectory dog was seen stealing meat off the carrier of an unattended bike, where did she retreat to enjoy her good fortune but into the grounds of the Catholic church?

The Church of Ireland rector and the Catholic parish priest are normally invited to local events of one kind or another. These range from senior citizens' Christmas parties, sporting events and festivals to blessing factories and offices. A certain parish priest who was asked to judge a bonny baby competition at a sports day insisted to the organisers that the rector do it jointly with him. He reasoned, rightly or wrongly, that if they both had a hand in the decision they were less likely to suffer the ire of the disappointed mothers than if he did it on his own.

One of the banks opened a new sub-office in Stradbally and Father Mahon and I were invited to bless it. Now I always had a problem about the theology of blessing buildings and other inanimate objects. The way round it is to pray that the building will be used for the benefit of the community and to pray for the people who will use it. On this occasion the building was a bank and since the Bible says that the love of money is the root of all evil, I felt myself in somewhat of a dilemma. Neither did my socialist principles allow me to approve too strenuously of what banks were up to. Conscious of my duty to represent the Church of Ireland community, however, I accepted the invitation and attended the opening.

After the bank manager spoke, outlining the marvellous service the bank was going to give the people of Stradbally, but without a word about the exorbitant profits he hoped to make out of them, he called on the parish priest to bless the new office. Father Mahon said a few words, pronounced a blessing and sprinkled holy water. The manager then called on me. I told the assembled company that I simply wished to draw their attention to two texts from the Bible, one from the Old Testament and one from the New. The first was, 'If wealth accumulates, set not your heart upon it.' And the second was to quote Our Lord himself who said, 'You cannot serve God and money.'

The most memorable public occasion while I was in Stradbally was the night President Childers came to Timahoe, at the invitation of the Athletic Club, to open their summer athletic festival. Father Dinny Doran, the curate in the village, was a big man, a larger than life character with a heart to match. We got on particularly well together. The village was *en fête*, grass cut, houses cleaned, painted and decorated for the visit. Dinny was master of ceremonies for the opening ceremony from the back of a lorry on the green in the centre of the village. Without a word of a note he stood up to welcome the President to Timahoe. He started off nervously but when he got into his stride, like a runaway horse, only exhaustion would stop him. Eventually he finished and called on me to speak. As I stood up to the microphone Dinny said in a stage whisper behind me, 'Pat, keep it short.'

After the opening, the President and the platform party, retired to Dinny's house for a sit down dinner, prepared and served by the members of the ICA. Dinny sat at the head of the long table with the President on his right. Mr Childers was not the easiest conversationalist in the world, so our host made the running when the going was tough. Dinny relaxed as the night went on with the help of a few balls of malt. At one point the President commented that he was afraid as he arrived in the village that the rain was about to come down, but didn't in the end.

'There was no danger in the world, Mr President,' said Dinny, 'the Holy Spirit and myself had that fixed.' As somebody down the table whispered, 'At least he put the Holy Spirit first.'

After the meal, in a gap in the conversation one of the committee stood up and took the opportunity to make a little speech and say what a great honour it was to be sitting at the same dinner table with the President of Ireland. Afraid of what might come next Dinny interrupted:

'Sit down, Paddy.' And turning to his distinguished guest said, 'Mr President, that's Paddy Fitzpatrick. Have you a woman round the Áras might suit him? Here he is in Timahoe wasting his sweetness on the desert air.' The President smiled, packed more tobacco into his pipe and said not a word.

The President's visit to Timahoe was a great success, and after we waved him off from the curate's house that night the party moved into another gear.

How Church of Ireland and Catholic clergy get on together in an area depends as much on congenial temperaments as on ecumenical attitudes. There are of course conservatives on both sides that do no more than the minimum. There are too, on both sides, ecumenical clergy who want to co-operate and do as much together as possible. As I suggested before, minorities are much more aware of what majorities stand for than the other way round. I was staggered by the extent that this was so one day walking past the Church of Ireland church with one of the Catholic curates in Stradbally, when he stopped to read the notice board inside the railing and said: 'What religion are you anyway?' I had been to this man's house for dinner and he had been to the rectory for dinner, yet he didn't know to which church I belonged.

The same man ran into trouble with the members of a youth club he started in his parish. I was sitting in my study one Saturday night when the doorbell rang. Three members of the Catholic parish youth club stood there and asked if they could speak to me. I invited them in.

'Could we come to your church in the morning?' they asked.

'Of course you can. Church of Ireland services are open to anyone who wants to come, but you had better tell me the story,' I said.

They had fallen out seriously with the curate over the way he ran the youth club and he had threatened to 'read them off the altar' next day. They planned that as soon as he started they would all get up as a body, walk out and across the street to the

Church of Ireland church. I tentatively suggested there might be a better way to make their protest. They didn't think so. While saying they were perfectly free to attend the Church of Ireland service I eventually persuaded them to handle the matter differently. Before they left they asked if on another Sunday they might come to the Church of Ireland service anyway just to see what it was like. Of course I said they could, but suggested that on the Sunday they were going to come they go first to Mass and also that they tell the curate what they were going to do. A few weeks later the three arrived at the service in Timogue Church. They had already been to Mass, but I suspect they didn't tell the curate. Their verdict was that the church was very plain, the service very simple and they were amazed how everybody in the church sang the hymns.

In September 1979 the Pope came to Ireland. It was the occasion of great celebration for the Catholic community. Many Church of Ireland people shared in the enthusiasm for the visit and went with their Catholic friends to see him. Shortly after the Pope left Ireland, a Church of Ireland parishioner arrived into the rectory to ask if there was some way we could make the most of the good feeling that had been engendered by his visit.

I fully supported the idea and invited Ned Aughney, the Catholic curate, to the rectory for coffee one morning and floated the idea. Ned was enthusiastic and we decided to start in a small way. We each hand-picked four parishioners and invited them to meet one evening a week for three weeks at the rectory to discuss ecumenism, with no conditions and no agenda.

On the first night the eight arrived slightly bemused at the vagueness of the invitation. All of them later confessed to having been nervous and one to having a stiff drink before he left home. The originator of the suggestion, one of the eight, outlined his idea and then Ned and I spoke about how Roman Catholicism and Anglicanism had much more in common than divided us. We named everything we shared and then listed the main points of doctrinal difference: papal infallibility, the Marian doctrines, justification by faith alone and so on. When the lay people saw how easily Ned and I could talk about these things, they relaxed and began to talk. They talked about their perceptions of difference.

'But you pray to statues.'

'Henry VIII started your church.'

'You confess your sins to the priest.'

'You don't believe in the Virgin Mary.'

Ned and I helped to refute all these half-truths and slowly, by the end of the three nights, a great bond had grown up among the members of the group, all of whom agreed that they could not just let it end there.

The original group met for another three nights to discuss particular issues that had arisen, while we started two more groups of eight. In due course we had clergy of both traditions with special interests, from outside the parish, to talk to larger groups. We got primary school teachers from the area together to talk about how they handled the issue of religious difference in school and, all in all, we created quite an ecumenical stir. People who knew each other as neighbours for years found they had more in common religiously than they thought and, where there was difference, there was a willingness to respect the other's point of view.

The Late Late Show got wind of what we were doing and sent a researcher, Mary O'Sullivan, down to investigate. She invited four of us on to the show one Saturday night where we got a great response from the audience. When I explained to Gay Byrne that Henry VIII did not start our religion and that we did of course believe in the Virgin Mary, and in fact we had three feast days to her in our church calendar, he said, 'We wuz conned.' We received letters from around the country approving heartily of what we were doing and saying we need more of this kind of thing. I also received a couple of abusive letters from the inevitable begrudgers.

When I went to Stradbally I transferred my Labour Party membership from Head Office to Portarlington Branch. I considered my political activity my own private affair. If as a citizen it was acceptable for me to vote it was in my view equally acceptable for me to be a member and work for a particular party. I did not conceal my political activity but I wanted to suss out Stradbally before I joined the local branch.

The redoubtable Ned Kelly dominated Portarlington branch. He was a character. A Labour Party member of the County Council, he was a law unto himself. He was outspoken, unpredictable and slightly eccentric, all calculated – it seemed to me – to promote himself first and the party second. He was committed to the principle that all publicity was good publicity. Reports in the local press of County Council meetings frequently carried accounts of something outlandish he said or did. When it came to one fund raising dance the tickets were printed as 'The Ned Kelly Dance' but that may have been at a time he had fallen out with the branch and considered himself Independent Labour. It was hard to keep track of Ned.

At one local government election he asked me to do a night's canvassing with him around Portarlington. I was not prepared to canvas in my parish. I was in mufti and drove. Ned planned the route. Our itinerary was all outside the town. When a door was opened Ned would say who he was and then introduce me with great relish as the Reverend Patrick Semple, rolling 'The Reverend' with his tongue for emphasis. In my naiveté it took me a few calls to tumble to the fact that Ned was bringing me to every Protestant farmer in the district and must have been disappointed I hadn't turned up in my collar.

Branch meetings were held in a back room in a pub in the square, where the proceedings were punctuated by the arrival of pints. I never drank at meetings but I would have one in the pub when the meeting was over, before I left. My high ideal that people should be politically involved to ensure Christian principles were employed in the political process was lost in the mass of the minutiae and the politics of the local branch. Much of our time was spent, with the help of Senator Jack Harte an organiser from Head Office, trying to re-organise the Laois division of the constituency.

During my time in Stradbally I was chairman of the Laois/ Offaly Constituency Council through two general elections. Approaching election time the blood is up and the knives are out. People who are not active at other times are interested and active. Potential nominees to run for election are watching their backs and their fronts and buying drinks for all and sundry. Approaching one of the general elections I had a telephone call from Barry Desmond to ask me if I would stand. I had no difficulty in saying immediately that I wasn't interested. Standing for election would conflict with my ministry and there was no contest. The Party's Administrative Council subsequently sent a representative, whose son, by sheer co-incidence, was a Church of Ireland clergyman, to ask me to reconsider. I didn't.

Clergy in parishes are a bit like bishops who never hear the truth again. The gossip circulates but the clergy are the last to hear it, if at all. My political involvement was well known as reports of branch elections and the like appeared in the local press. I did not initiate political discussion with parishioners on principle and nobody did so with me. I was doubly careful of what I said in sermons so that nobody could accuse me of using my position to promote my political beliefs.

On a routine parish visit one day a farmer parishioner said to me: 'It's strange you should call today. I had a visit this morning from a gentleman canvassing my support for a petition to have you removed from the parish. I put him out of the yard.'

He told me who it was. It was a parishioner who had never spoken to me on the matter of my political involvement. The same parishioner had called to the rectory a few days before this to collect a message and was perfectly civil, but said nothing to me of his problem with my political activity. When I got home there was another parishioner waiting for me to warn me that the said gentleman was on the warpath. I expected a visit from the man himself but it never materialised. Later I discovered that he had been in touch with my predecessor as rector, who gave him no encouragement.

At a parish meeting subsequently, my political involvement

was raised. I outlined my position, saying it was my own private business and I did not want in any way to involve the parish or parishioners. There were rumblings of discontent that were extinguished by a few well-chosen words from the only tradesman amongst the group of prosperous farmers. 'There wouldn't be a word about the rector's political involvement if he was a member of Fine Gael,' he said. I grinned internally and had no further need to defend myself at that particular meeting.

The certain gentleman on the warpath was not to be deterred. Still without a word to me, he went to see my bishop but got no satisfaction there. This was still not enough. He turned up late at the Parish Annual General meeting and from the door berated me and called on me to desist from politics. I invited him to join the meeting to have his say but he would not. His father was sitting in the front row and asked me gently the intelligent and pertinent question: 'Is there any conflict between your membership of the Labour Party and being rector of this parish?' I thanked him for his courtesy and answered, 'There is no conflict whatever between the two.' I never heard another word of the matter.

The rectory was in the village. It was in grounds of over an acre, with a stable yard with coach house and a 'haggard', used in the days when the rector farmed the glebe land himself as part of his stipend. Up to ten or fifteen years previously the then rector still kept a cow for the house. There was a large orchard now neglected and overgrown but most of the trees still bore good fruit. Some of the best fruit was virtually inaccessible because of mountains of briars growing around them. This, however, was not a deterrent to the boys who lived in the council houses up the avenue. Like the rectory in Wexford, the orchard was not visible from the house but we could hear when the boys were in to help themselves – poetic justice. We only disturbed them, but with no intention of catching them, if they came when the apples were not yet ripe.

How could one small family be entitled to all those apples when so many families up the road had none? So when the apples were at their height we used to give bags of apples to the women, glad that they would be used and not wasted, but this was no use to the boys. They still came in over the fence at the lower end. Twenty years later I met a man who had been a boy in Stradbally when I was there. I remembered him well.

'I suppose you were one of the ones that used to come in to rob the orchard.'

He grinned sheepishly.

'I was,' he said.

I told him we used to know when the boys were in the orchard.

He laughed but he was surprised and probably disappointed to hear that his childhood escapades were less heroic than he thought.

In earlier times there was a full-time man to keep the grounds. Those days were gone and the best we could do was to keep the area around the house. On my day off there was nothing I liked better than to don old clothes and hack back the wilderness.

One day I was up on the high perimeter wall cutting back ivy when I heard a voice below me on the footpath.

'Howa'ya?'

I looked down to see a small boy of about six looking up.

'I'm fine. How are you?'

'What are you doing?'

'I'm cutting ivy.'

'Why are you doing that?'

'Because if I don't it'll damage the wall.'

There was a long silence. Then the voice said:

'I drink stout you know.'

'You don't,' I said, 'You're too young to drink stout.'

All the time I was working away, being careful not to fall off the wall.

I looked down and the boy was gone.

Five minutes later I heard the little voice again.

'I'm back.'

I looked down and there he was, an open bottle of stout in his hand putting it to his mouth.

'Where did you get that?' I asked.

'Me Da keeps them under the sink.'

I thought for a while and for something to say I said:

'Who is your teacher in school?'

'Sister Michael.'

'Does she know you drink stout?'

'She don't, and if you tell her I'll give you a kick up the arse.'

In Stradbally we were very much part of the whole village community in a way a Church of Ireland rector would not have been in former years. We were particularly friendly with one family who gave excellent dinner parties. After dinner Father Hughes, an old friend of the family, would preside at the piano and entertain the party for the rest of the evening and into the small hours. He was wont to accompany himself to a rendition of 'The Sash', which was followed by the local Church of Ireland rector singing 'Kevin Barry', learned years before in the bar of Leinster Cricket Club.

CHAPTER TWELVE

The College and West Wicklow

In the past the average Church of Ireland adult member's formal learning in the faith ended at confirmation at about the age of fourteen. In Church of Ireland managed National Schools children were taught by professionals, but in Sunday Schools many teachers were amateurs, untrained in their subject or in teaching. Clergy normally taught confirmation class and, though trained in their subject, were mostly untrained in teaching children. In recent years there have been some changes. Today training is available for Sunday School teachers and clergy get a little training in teaching before ordination. After confirmation most adults have learned some Bible stories, some hymns and some important parts of the catechism. Since confirmation was a long time ago for adults, many have forgotten much of what they learned.

The question arises then, 'Do adults need to know more?' If they attend their church and participate regularly in worship, is this not enough? Most people, including many clergy, would answer yes to this. What is more, the numbers of those who are in church Sunday by Sunday are counted and these numbers are the main criterion by which the success or otherwise of a parish are judged – bums on pews.

During my time in Stradbally, the Church of Ireland formed an Adult Education Council. They approached me to spend some time as part-time officer to the Council to promote adult education in the church at large. By this time I was well settled in Stradbally and since it was a small parish I agreed, with the permission of my bishop, to give two days a week to adult education.

If adult education had been a priority for the church, and if there had been plenty of money available, the ideal would have been to select someone, send them off for a couple of years to train and qualify in adult Christian education and come back and work full-time in the church. Unfortunately the Church of Ireland does not operate that way. To be fair, it has neither the personnel available nor the money, so it has to improvise as best it can.

I soon discovered that the image most people had of adult education was motorbike maintenance and flower arranging at evening class in the local 'tech'. The idea that there was a need for adult Christian education in the church to help people to grow and develop in their faith, to help them to relate their faith to life experience and life experience to their faith, was new to most people. It was my job to convince clergy and lay people, who saw church attendance alone as the criterion of church membership, of the need for people to grow and develop in faith, and it was my job to provide the means to do it.

I read voraciously in adult Christian education and set about discovering what other churches were doing in this area. Learning as I went along, I taught adult education to ordinands in their pastoral training and helped some clergy to set up adult education events in their parishes. There was a limit to how much I could do in two days a week while all the time the Adult Education Council planned and politicked to have a full-time officer. In the fullness of time the church's Priorities Fund financed a full-time appointment that was advertised by the Council. Interviews were held and I was appointed to the full-time post.

I left Stradbally after eleven years and took up the Adult Education Officer post, based at the Divinity Hostel that by now had become the Church of Ireland Theological College. My brief was to teach adult education to all three years of theological students, to run in-service training for clergy and to help clergy to develop adult learning projects in their parishes. A formidable task.

I was fascinated to return to Braemor Park fifteen years after I had been a student there myself. I found the same diversity of students and the same dynamics operating between them. If anything, there were more evangelicals and they were more hard line. They observed, some reluctantly, the requirements for worship of the college insofar as they were obliged to, but held their own little prayer meetings where I discovered they prayed for my conversion and presumably for the conversion of other members of the staff and students who held a different theological position from theirs. After one address I gave in the college chapel a student slipped a tract under the door of my office entitled 'How to Become a Christian'.

There were fundamentalists who resented any form of biblical criticism. It was not uncommon for some of these students to contradict flatly the professors and lecturers in biblical studies in Trinity where they did their academic work. They came to college wet behind the ears from recent conversion experiences and knew it all. They brought their Bibles to lectures, including adult education lectures, to find texts to confound or confirm what the lecturer said. They knew well those parts of the Bible that supported their own position, but then I suppose to some extent we are all guilty of quoting scripture to re-enforce us in our prejudices. Shakespeare had it right again: 'The devil can cite scripture for his purpose.'

The hope was that students, during their time in college, would learn more about the Bible and its place in the life of the church. The rectors of the home parishes of some students helped to confound this objective by telling them that when they went to the Theological College they should learn what they must of biblical criticism and later on disregard it. Some, however, over their three years did develop in their understanding of the Bible and in their own theological thinking.

As in my time, there was a small number of 'high church' students who were anathema to the fundamentalists who saw them as under the influence of Rome. The 'high church' students emphasised the Catholic side of Anglicanism and gave a high place to ritual in worship. The rest of the students were in the middle, various shades of broad and liberal. In fact what I'm saying is no more than that the college reflected the diversity of the shades of Anglicanism represented in the church. It was just the same as when I was a student.

I enjoyed teaching, despite the fact that some of the students thought that I mightn't be a Christian at all. I found the atmosphere of the college suffocating at times and was glad I did not live in. You can get too much of a good thing.

I particularly enjoyed in-service training for clergy. After years in pastoral ministry, some clergy were glad to reflect on what they were doing and explore some of the issues that arose from a study of adult Christian education. Together for a weekend they were generally prepared to be honest in the group. I tried to introduce them to perspectives on their ministry that would help them to clarify what they were doing and why; to help them to establish priorities for their parishes. The work of clergy is so all consuming and diverse that it is important that unspoken assumptions are explored and real priorities established.

The very word 'parish' has given a word to the English language, 'parochial', meaning 'restricted or confined within narrow limits, possessing a narrowness of view'. This well describes the prevailing mentality of many parishes. I tried to give to clergy the rudiments of how to run adult education events in their parishes in such a way as to broaden people's view of the parish and its work. I also made myself available to go out into parishes to work with clergy and lay people at exploring their faith in the context of their parish life.

You would think that in a job like Adult Education Officer one might be free of fund raising, but no. The Council decided to establish a video library to make available good church related videos. The trouble was there was no money so I set about raising some. We needed three video recorders and TVs. I first convinced my own bank, the Ulster, to provide one of each, promising to put a little plate on them to say 'Supplied by The Ulster Bank Ltd'. The Bible tells us to be 'Wise as serpents and gentle as doves,' so I wrote very gentle letters to both the Bank of Ireland and AIB to tell them what the Ulster Bank had done. I had replies from both to say that they too would supply the same.

I was answerable in all I did in the college to the Principal, and for my work out in the church I was responsible to the Adult Education Council. I had the support of both, which was encouraging. In sitting on the Adult Education Council and being *ex officio* in attendance at the Church of Ireland Board of Education, its parent body, for the first time I gained insights into the workings of the Church of Ireland in some of its central committees. I did not enjoy this committee work which was largely run by 'professional' committee people who seemed to relish it.

The General Synod, whose work between its annual meetings is conducted by an elected Standing Committee, runs the Church of Ireland. It has subsidiary Boards, of which the Board of Education is one, to run various aspects of the church's life. Then there is the Representative Church Body that administers the trust under which the church's main finance is held. These and other central committees are broadly representative of the church at large and their members give time and a great deal of effort to run them. In fact many of the decision-making processes of the church are in the hands of a small number of people, some of whom indulge in politics, manipulation and manoeuvring in order to ensure that things are done their way.

Some lay people give a great deal of their time to this work and it is incontrovertible that someone has to do it but I found my limited experience of these committees entirely uncongenial. I was more at ease at branch meetings of the Labour Party. There is deep down somewhere inside us the expectation that the church as an institution, because it is the church, should behave differently from other institutions. We expect that all the church's deliberations and actions should take place according to the fundamental principles of Christianity. I'm not sure if church boards and committees at any level are more likely to observe Christian principles than any others. The church as an institution is made up of the same fallible human beings and is bound to be subject to the same human motivations and ambitions, gifts and failings as any other institution. Just as ordination does not confer perfection on clergy, so lay people on church committees are no different from people on committees anywhere. Nor, perhaps, should we expect them to be.

The church is obliged by its constitution to provide a residence for its rectors. This principle is extended to specialist officers and so I was provided with a house in Templeogue. It is galling to hear people saying things like 'Clergy may not be paid very well, but aren't they lucky to have a fine free house.' I make no comment on the stipend, but for clergy the free house during their working life is not a blessing but a curse. First of all, while living in a rectory they must go cap in hand to a local committee of sixteen or more people to have things done to the house that are necessary, and often overdue, to keep it in reasonable order as a family home. When retirement comes they leave their fine free house with nothing but their furniture. Unless from private means they can provide somewhere to live, they must rent somewhere out of their modest pension if they are not to rely on charity.

When I was in Stradbally an elderly clergyman in the diocese retired. A farmer parishioner gave him the corner of a field in which to put a mobile home for himself and his sister who lived with him. He may not have been very provident during his working life, but to provide a house from his stipend was difficult if not impossible.

If a clergyman dies in service, his widow can have as little as a few months to make place for his successor and find somewhere to live for herself and her family. These days with scarcity of clergy most parishes, however, take much longer to fill. The church does make a substantial grant to a widow but not enough to buy a house. Some clergy widows live in council houses. 'And why not?' you may say and rightly so; no reason why not if this is their choice, but let nobody say a free house during the working life of their husband is a blessing. If the clergy were paid enough to start a mortgage and provide their own house, retired clergy and widows would have some security.

The committees at the centre do an excellent job with the finance available to support retired clergy and widows, but it is not a bonus to have a free house.

Towards the end of my second three-year term, I had had enough of Adult Christian Education. I missed parish life and the direct contact with parishioners and families. I applied for and was appointed in due course as rector of the vacant parish of Donoughmore and Donard with Dunlavin in West Wicklow. The fact that nobody was appointed to succeed me as Adult Education Officer was a measure of the Church of Ireland's commitment to adult education. During my time as Officer, the Adult Education Council published a handbook to which the Primate Dr Eames wrote a foreword. He said:

> It is impossible to overestimate the importance of Adult Education for the Church of Ireland. I am increasingly conscious that we need to give great attention to this aspect of our work.

One year later, when I resigned as Adult Education Officer to go back to a parish, the Board of Education refused to appoint a successor. Just as it was beginning to gain ground, adult education in the church went steadily down hill. Recently the Standing Committee of the General Synod abolished the Adult Education Council altogether.

The Donoughmore and Donard end of my new parish was the Glen of Imaal, bounded to the east by the Wicklow Mountains, dominated by Lugnaquilla, and to the west by the main Blessington-Baltinglass Road. The Dunlavin end of the parish was on the west side of this road. The two had formerly been separate parishes that had come together in the recent past. It takes generations for the component parts of a united parish to develop a common identity. Very few parishioners will be happy to go to another of the churches in a parish other than their own. Each group perceives the other somehow as a threat and they keep very much to themselves. The Christian principle 'Love your neighbour as yourself' doesn't seem to carry the same weight for some people when parishes amalgamate.

There was a high concentration of Church of Ireland people in the area and with three churches, two National Schools and two parish halls, and all that goes with renovating and maintaining and running them, there was no shortage of work to be done, apart altogether from the normal liturgical and pastoral duties. The parish raised large sums of money to renovate buildings and the energy that parishioners at both ends of the parish expended on fund raising was remarkable. Despite the fact that there is no reference to this kind of 'estate management' in theological college, in the ordination service, or in the service of institution to a parish, it takes up a large amount of a rector's time. It takes up a large amount of parishioners' time too in addition to their daily work. Despite this expenditure of energy on money and buildings, there is a good spin off. Parishioners working together in this way create *esprit de corps* that is good for the parish.

Since parishioners had spent so much money on buildings – churches, halls and schools – for themselves, they decided to have Lent fund raising projects to do something for somebody else. The parish raised over £4,000 in each of three Lents. One project was to ship a Land Rover to a third world farm in Africa and provide the balance of the £4,000 in cash for the farm. Another £4,000 went to fitting a kitchen for a Simon Community centre in Dublin, and the third project provided a special bed for the hospice on the Curragh. These projects were the 'Love your neighbour' bit of Jesus' injunction 'Love your neighbour as yourself.' Computed in financial terms, we didn't in fact love our neighbour quite as much as we loved ourselves.

Ecumenical relations at both ends of the parish were good. Lay people got on well and Father Kevin Lyon and I worked well together. He invited Hilary and me to comment on and in due course to proof-read a book on the psalms that he published. When he was transferred to Blessington, Father Paddy Finn arrived as his replacement.

Paddy turned out to be the most unselfconscious and natural ecumenist I ever met and became a good friend. His nature was to reach out to cross divides, to bring people together and to give confidence to his own parishioners and to mine to do together as much as we could. Apart from his natural instinct as an ecumenist, he had studied at the School of Ecumenics and had a particular interest in the Lambeth Quadrilateral. He also had a special affection for the prophet Habbakuk. The Lambeth Quadrilateral is a late nineteenth-century statement from the Anglican standpoint of the essentials for a reunited Christian church.

On Paddy's suggestion we dropped the traditional ecumenical service in the Week of Prayer for Christian Unity, since it had run its course, and which only a handful of worthy souls attended. We replaced it with a pilgrimage on a summer Sunday afternoon to the top of Church Mountain in the parish where there was a church ruin. On the top we had some prayers and sang a hymn and returned to one of the fields below for a picnic. Robert Dunlop, the Baptist pastor from Brannockstown, also joined in this event. As many as ten times the numbers who used to attend the service came on the walk, which created a great opportunity for people to come together.

When Paddy and I had an inter-church marriage between our parishioners we made it a principle, apart from sharing in the service together, to arrive at the church together in the car of one or other of us, and then go to the house of either to spend that dreadful time when the photographer is doing his best or worst at the hotel and the guests are filling the coffers of the hotel bar. We then arrived together at the hotel just in time for the meal and left together afterwards.

Over the years my struggles with aspects of faith did not get easier. I eventually stopped trying to discuss things with clergy friends and colleagues, since none of them admitted to similar problems. I was never sure that this was because they didn't have difficulties of belief or that they had them and weren't prepared to admit to them. I suspect that they didn't have the doubting Thomas temperament that I had. Some people seem to buy the package of Christianity and never unpack it to work with what is inside. In the ministry it is easy to become so involved in one's work and in the life of the church at large that there is no time to think about matters of belief.

My conscience got to such a pitch at one stage during my time in Donoughmore and Dunlavin, and such was my struggle with faith, that I felt I had to tell my bishop, Archbishop Caird, what I did believe and what I did not believe. If he said I had to go, so be it. I had no idea what I would do or where I would go but I felt I had to talk to him. I made an appointment and told him where I stood. D. A. R. Caird has a good mind, a short fuse and a quick sense of humour. He is more likely to quote the rubrics, the canons and the Constitution than the Bible. He was not shocked when I told him where I stood; given the man he was I did not expect him to be. On the contrary, we had a theological discussion for the best part of an hour after which, in so many words, he told me to get back to work. I was relieved that I was not outside, not least since I had no other way of earning a living. It is peculiar that I have heard of clergy leaving the ministry for many reasons but never for loss of faith. I wonder why?

About two years later a certain rector from another diocese phoned me out of the blue and asked me to meet him. We met for coffee when he recounted exactly where he stood theologically. He was very close to where I was and I found this reassuring. He too found it good to talk to a kindred spirit.

I was always careful not to try to impose my way of looking at faith matters on other people, especially in sermons or in discussions with parishioners. I didn't want to end up at the bottom of the sea tied to a millstone! I would not want to injure anyone's faith but there are lay people for whom some aspects of the faith are incredible and they need to be taken account of too. In fact in the parish there was a small group of parishioners who found a new approach to interpreting belief helpful. People who had had difficulties of belief for years and kept quiet about it for fear of being thought odd, until they heard a clergyman giving rise to some of the same questions. If I pointed to a different way of understanding something I was always careful to give the traditional way too. I would say: 'You may find this way of looking at it makes sense for you, but if you find the traditional way more helpful, well then stay with that.'

For example, the traditional way to understand the birth narratives of Jesus in the gospels is that the events recounted – the annunciation, the stable, the shepherds and choir of angels, the wise men, and so on – happened as recounted in the New Testament. That they were actual historical events. It is more likely, however, that the narratives were stories written after Jesus had departed, to convey the truth of who the early church believed Jesus was. A story to give a beginning to the life of the man they knew as an adult and to reflect what they believed about him. What is important is not what happened but what it means. In other words, you don't have to believe the story literally or historically in order for the writer to convey that he believed that Jesus was the Son of God. The early Christians were not convinced that Jesus was the Son of God because they knew he didn't have a human father. They were convinced because of what they knew of his life, death and resurrection. What they knew of him did not depend on historical detail. Conveying religious truths in this way by story or myth was a common device in the ancient world.

The important thing is the truth conveyed, not the means of doing it. I believe that people should be free to understand the birth narratives either way. Many clergy have no difficulty accepting the story method but baulk at telling their lay people about it for fear of damaging their faith if they are told the events recounted may not actually have happened. I believe that this is to underestimate lay people and their faith. The insights of biblical criticism have been around for over 100 years but have largely been kept inside the walls of academia. Some fundamentalists reject biblical criticism altogether. Those clergy who do not, are often disinclined to pass on its methods and insights to lay people for fear they may disturb their faith. It is surprising how many highly intelligent and educated lay people, working at the highest levels of their professions, when it comes to their religion are in junior infants. It is the clergy's job to change this, but as long as these lay people simply continue to attend church, many clergy don't seem to want to help them to grow and develop in their faith.

On the other hand there are, I believe, many people who don't have anything to do with the church because they find a literal approach to Christianity incredible. If these people had been taught an understanding of the biblical accounts from the insights of biblical criticism, many of them might not have left the church in the first place.

CHAPTER THIRTEEN

Dublin Again

Until about the 1950s it was not uncommon for clergy to stay in parishes for forty or more years. Some of the old rectors used to say clergy should stay in a parish until they are baptising the grandchildren of those they first married. It is uncommon these days to find a rector who has been in a parish for more than twenty years. But in recent times clergy movement is slowing up again because so many clergy wives work and don't want to leave their jobs, and children of clergy don't want to move schools.

The system of appointment to parishes is, like many things in the Church of Ireland, on the face of it democratic. When a parish becomes vacant a Board of Nomination is convened, as stipulated in the Constitution. It consists of lay people, at least two of whom are from the vacant parish, clergy from the diocese and the bishop is chairman. The Board usually advertises the vacancy in church publications and Board members are free to put names forward. Clergy who are interested may apply. These days, for 'plum' city parishes there may be a dozen or more names considered, while for small country parishes nobody suitable may be found willing to go there and the parish may be vacant for a few years. The bishop cannot move clergy around at will but if a Board of Nomination does not nominate to the bishop within three months the nomination to that parish is at the discretion of the bishop himself.

Some clergy move more often than others for all kinds of reasons. One rector, who moved every three to four years over his career, was deemed by his colleagues to have a slight weakness: he collected colour televisions! Some rectors want to move but cannot find a suitable vacant parish or, having found one, they are not appointed. There have been a couple of cases of clergy returning to parishes where they had been rector some years previously. It is an uneven and unpredictable process that allows plenty of room for the work of the Holy Spirit.

After eight years in West Wicklow the opportunity for an interesting job arose. Apart from my first curacy I had served in country parishes. A small Dublin inner city parish, St George and St Thomas, was coming vacant, which included chaplaincies to three hospitals, The Mater, The Mater Private and Temple Street Children's Hospital and the chaplaincy to Mountjoy Prison. I had never been in the inner city, nor had I been a hospital or prison chaplain before and I was ready for a change. It was a bishop's appointment and I accepted the offer.

St George's Church in Hardwicke Place, a landmark in the north inner city, was now a concert hall and the small congregation of mostly elderly people attended St Thomas' Church in Cathal Brugha Street. To a person they were a dedicated group of parishioners. There was nothing they would not do for their parish and their church. They were the remnant of what had been one of the most fashionable parishes in the nineteenth century when the professional and social elite of Dublin lived in Mountjoy Square and surrounding area. The remnant were however true-blue 'Dubs', as Dublin as Phoenix Park and proud of it. They were proud of their parish and their distinctive tradition, sad at their diminishing numbers but determined to soldier on. As recently as the early nineteen sixties they remembered having to go early to St George's to be sure of a seat at a Harvest Thanksgiving or Carol Service, two special occasions in any Church of Ireland parish. Over the years families had moved out to the suburbs and left behind a handful determined to survive.

St Thomas' Church replaced a previous church on the site that had been destroyed during the Civil War. It was dedicated in 1931 when it would have been full on Sunday mornings. Now the small group came faithfully to morning service. There was one midweek communion, and a parish bowls club used the church one night a week during the winter.

St Thomas' Church is a fine building, strategically placed a few paces from the city's main thoroughfare, O'Connell Street. Since the church was used only minimally, the parish decided, in an attempt to make it more widely available, to have lunchtime talks once a week in the month of October, given by notable people on the theme 'I Believe ...' The talks were designed so that people working in the area could attend in their lunchtime. We approached the DIT opposite the church to see if someone from the catering department would provide a soup and rolls lunch after the talks. Jim Bowe, one of the chefs, came forward delighted to help. We did not charge for lunch but invited voluntary contributions that we gave at the end of each series to different inner city charities.

Between two and three hundred people came to the talks to hear what celebrities such as Maeve Binchy, Brendan Kennelly, Garret FitzGerald, Vincent Browne, John Lonergan and others had to say. It was fascinating to hear what diverse approaches the guest speakers took to the topic 'I Believe ...' Some were orthodox Christian, some were non-believers and believed passionately in other things, and one humanist, Emer O'Kelly, expressed with great integrity and good humour some views that were not exactly complimentary to the church. After each talk there was time for questions that gave rise to many interesting topics.

The response of some people invited to speak was fascinating. I spent ten minutes on the phone trying to convince Tony Gregory, a TD for the area, to take part. I tried every trick I knew to convince him but failed. He would debate political questions with anyone but he did not feel he could make a ten-minute presentation, even on his political beliefs, to a live audience. One nationally known broadcaster, who shall be nameless, declined to take part on the grounds that her job was asking questions, not making statements. One year she did, however, give generous airtime on her programme to publicise the talks. Vincent Browne, when he arrived at the church and saw it full, took the Lord's name in shock and stumbled nervously through the first few minutes of his script before settling down. It seems that some people who are used to talking to microphones are unnerved at the prospect of talking to a large group of real live people.

Parishioners were delighted with members of the public coming to their church for the talks. Conversely, people were equally delighted to see inside the church that many of them passed regularly for years and believed to be closed.

The hospital chaplaincy work I learned from the beginning with the help of my colleagues, the Catholic chaplains. I was warmly welcomed to each of the three hospitals by management and chaplains, all of whom were tremendously supportive. Hospital chaplaincy has become a specialised ministry with a specialised training that more Church of Ireland clergy and lay people are now doing. There is a Clinical Pastoral Education training centre at the Mater Hospital for training chaplains, and both Fr Dermot Brennan and Sister Louisa Ritchie, the two supervisors during my time there, invited me to conduct seminars with students on Anglicanism and the Church of Ireland. Furthermore CPE Ireland co-opted me onto its Board. These events are an indication of important ecumenical developments on the ground.

Before I was appointed chaplain to Mountjoy I needn't tell you I knew it only from the outside – the shot of the front gate that appears on television news. It was built in the mid-nineteenth century and has been in continuous use ever since, and it shows. It is in a state of neglect. My initial impression on first entering Mountjoy was the noise. When prisoners are out of their cells on the landings the decibel level is high.

As a newcomer, the governor and prison authorities and chaplains at Mountjoy equally warmly received their new Church of Ireland chaplain. Just as at the hospitals, they supported and encouraged me as I learned the ropes and came to terms with working in a strange environment. The question I was asked most often when people heard I was a prison chaplain was: 'Are there many Church of Ireland prisoners in Mountjoy?' There weren't many indigenous Church of Ireland prisoners from Foxrock or Howth, in fact as you know damned well there weren't any. There were, however, a few from some of the socially deprived areas of the city. It's strange how criminals from affluent areas don't tend to end up in prison while those from poor areas do.

I had on my list up to twenty prisoners at any one time, some from Ireland but mainly Anglicans from the UK and abroad. Their offences were right across the board but most were in for drug offences and credit card and other kinds of fraud. Sister Mary Slattery, one of my chaplain colleagues, insisted that I dealt with a better class of prisoner!

There are two extreme attitudes to prisoners: 'Lock 'em up and throw away the key,' and 'There but for the grace of God go I.' I am firmly in the latter camp. I have absolutely no doubt that if I had the start in life that most prisoners in Mountjoy had I might not have been half as good as they, and if most prisoners had the start in life that I had, they might have made twice as much of it as I did. The connection between family and social deprivation and crime is incontrovertible. Before you try to disprove this by quoting the exceptions, of course not everyone who suffered early deprivation ends up in prison, but it is clear that the majority of those who do end up in prison come from socially deprived areas.

Of course some people should be in prison, including some wealthy people who defraud the Revenue Commissioners and commit other white collar crimes, but the answer to crime is not to build more prison places but to address the social environment that fosters crime. It has been shown in other countries that more prison places do not reduce crime. It beggars belief that a Minister for Justice and a government can be so stupid as to waste taxpayers' money on building more prisons, rather than investing that money to address the social problems that incubate crime. The folly of building more prison places is not about solving the problem. It is about votes.

On average there were ten or fifteen prisoners at chapel on Sunday mornings. None of them were churchgoers before being sentenced, and I doubt very much if any of them would be a churchgoer after discharge. But they did value chapel while in prison as a quiet place to which to come apart. One female prisoner asked for baptism and confirmation. After preparation, the ceremony was conducted in Archbishop Empey's private chapel at his house. Afterwards Mrs Empey entertained us all to tea in the drawing room. Two men asked for confirmation and on separate occasions the archbishop came into the prison chapel to confirm them. In each case the governor attended a tea and bun reception for all involved after the service. For one of these services the mother, brother and grandmother of the prisoner came over from the UK for the occasion.

To be in prison is simply awful – to be deprived of one's freedom; to be powerless over one's own life; to be subject to the necessities of prison order; to be locked up in a cell sixteen hours a day. If cells were carpeted, had colour TVs and stereos and if they each had en suite showers, none of which they have, prison would still be awful. Try locking yourself in your own bedroom for sixteen hours a day for a few days and see how you get on.

The job of the prison chaplain is to be present with the powerless, to encourage the prisoner's self worth, which for most prisoners is very low, if there at all. It is not for the chaplain to trivialise the crime or to be judgmental, that is the job of the courts. Jesus told us, 'Judge not that you be not judged.' The anonymous bard put it:

There's good in the worst of us,

And bad in the best of us,

And it ill behoves any of us

To speak ill of the rest of us.

The chaplain's job is to affirm the prisoner. The prisoner is in no doubt what the chaplain stands for. There is no need to preach or pontificate. As Christians we are called to give unconditional love, and leave the rest to God.

After two and a half years at St Thomas' I retired, which gave time for the foregoing ruminations. Working in the ordained ministry is like any job – there are the good bits, the difficult bits, the routine bits and the boring bits. Overall it is a satisfying life. Unless you misbehave or lose the faith completely, you'll never be out of a job. It is very satisfying working with people, and sometimes it is immensely frustrating. The old saying holds true for the ministry: 'You can please all the people some of the time, some of the people all of the time, but you cannot please all the people all the time.' And you'd be a fool to try.

Epilogue

Christians of all traditions claim to follow faithfully the teaching of Jesus Christ. By Christian I mean Roman Catholic, Anglican, Presbyterian, Methodist, Baptist and the myriad of other Protestant groups and Gospel Halls that exist worldwide. It is central to the teaching of many of these that they and they alone are the true Church of Jesus Christ, and by definition every other Christian group is to a greater or lesser extent defective.

In medieval times the church considered it to be its duty to 'point out' to people whose beliefs were contrary to that of the official church that they were in error. They did this by imprisoning them, torturing them, gouging out their eyes and maiming them and by burning them at the stake. In England in the sixteenth century a Catholic queen burned Protestants and a Protestant queen burned Catholics. In Spain 'inquisition', the routing out and punishment of heretics, continued until as late as 1820.

In more recent times authorities responsible for taking sanctions against false doctrine toned down their punishments. The penal laws simply made it illegal for Roman Catholics to practise their religion. Their ownership of property and access to education and the professions were forbidden or restricted.

Today official sanctions are rare but prejudice between Christians is rife. In Northern Ireland bitterness and hatred between Christians have led to community strife, murder and war. If the churches had addressed religious apartheid in the north of Ireland over the years, would we have had the bitterness, hatred and bloodshed of the past thirty years? For too long the churches seemed content to live in their own ghettos, looking across at the others with anything from suspicion to hatred, largely engendered by ignorance of each other. Only when the Troubles broke out and things got out of hand was there a serious attempt by Protestant and Catholic clergy to build bridges.

Throughout history religion has been as much, if not more, a curse than a blessing. It had as much chance, if not more chance, of leading to division, bitterness and hatred as it had of leading to coming together, trust and love. There are signs that churches and individual Christians are coming to their senses at last. The building of bridges, the establishing of trust and the doing of things together are all happening more and more. There is more mutual respect for different points of view. We are all maturing. To be able to live comfortably with diversity is a sign of maturity for both individuals and communities. The converse is also true: to be threatened by diversity is a sign of immaturity.

Jesus is recorded in the New Testament as having said: 'Love your enemies', 'Do good to those who despitefully use you', 'Turn the other cheek', 'Forgive seventy times seven'. He summed up all of his teaching in 'Love God and love your neighbour as yourself.' The church and Christians over the years, who were responsible for some appalling atrocities, must have thought that when Jesus said all these things he was only joking. Bigoted and bitter Christians today must think the same.

There is something deep down in us that makes us want to be right, or perhaps it is that we don't want to be wrong. So having the truth excludes those who differ from us and when others are excluded we don't have to bother about them. They are lesser beings than us. Our job is either to try to get them to become like us, or at best to ignore them, or at worst exercise some kind of prejudice or sanction against them.

'See how these Christians love one another,' was originally said about the early church when pagans noticed how Christians genuinely loved each other. Today it is used sarcastically about Christians when they hate each other.

Furthermore, the institutional church hijacked the gospel of love and turned it into an instrument for exercising power and control over its own members, and used the threat of hell and the reward of heaven to do it. If you inculcate children with guilt early enough in their lives you then make them dependent on the means of salvation over which you have control and which you dispense. If you don't do what I tell you as a means to purge your guilt, or if you don't do it my way, you will go to hell. In other words you control people by fear of punishment. Churches have used life after death as a threat. God was portrayed as a tyrannical judge rather than as a loving father.

It is unfortunate that in English there is one word 'love' to cover all kinds of love: parental love, filial love, romantic love, erotic love, and Christian love. In other languages there are different words for different kinds of love. In Greek the word for Christian love is *agape*, meaning costly self-giving love. Christian love is not, as some people feel, weak and sentimental. It is based on the recognition of one's own human fallibility, the acceptance of human failing in others and above all the capacity to forgive. The exercise of Christian love is the capacity to treat the other with the same acceptance and forgiveness that one would want for oneself, if one is genuinely humble enough to acknowledge that one needs forgiveness.

Some people delude themselves that not only have they got the truth but also that they have the whole truth. They believe truth is strong and when you have it you are inviolable. Love, on the other hand, they see as weak, leaving one vulnerable, which of course is true because you cannot love unless you are vulnerable.

Purity of doctrine has in the past been pursued at the expense of Christian love. How Christians who claim to have unique access to the truth of Christianity can consistently behave without Christian love when it is central to the truth of the gospel, I do not know.

Of course the churches must deal in theological truths but they must implement these truths with love, not with arrogance, exclusiveness and pride. It is a matter of speaking the truth in love. For too long the love was absent. There are real signs that this is changing.